I0160981

SUPPLEMENT EDITION

SAPPHO: THE POEMS

prepared by the translator
Sasha Newborn

BANDANNA BOOKS   2011   SANTA BARBARA

Supplement Edition: Sappho: The Poems copyright © 1996 Bandanna Books.
ISBN 0-942208-40-4

BANDANNA BOOKS COLLEGE TITLES

Sappho: The Poems.* Greece's greatest lyric poet. $9.95

Areopagitica: Freedom of the Press.* John Milton.
Censorship history ancient and modern. $9.95

The Apology of Socrates, & The Crito.* Plato. $9.95

The First Detective: Three Stories. Edgar Allan Poe.
Poe's amateur detective Dupin was
the model for Sherlock Holmes. $12.95

Don't Panic: The Procrastinator's Guide to Writing
an Effective Term Paper. Steven Posusta. $11.95

Mitos y Leyendas de México/Myths and Legends of Mexico.
Luis Leal. Twenty origin stories and history.
Color plates by Álvaro Ángel Suman. $39.50

Ghazals of Ghalib. Ghalib's witty couplets,
arguing with God, his beloved. $9.95

The Merchant of Venice. William Shakespeare. Art by
Orson Welles. Edited by Rachel Burke. $11.95

Gandhi on the Gita. M.K. Gandhi explains the
Bhagavad Gita chapter by chapter. $9.95

Leaves of Grass, 1855 edition.*
Walt Whitman. $11.95

Italian for Opera Lovers. Italian opera terms. $5.95

Dante & His Circle. D. G. Rossetti. Italian love
sonnets & Dante's Vita Nuova. $12.95

Order through our website at www.bandannabooks.com/bbooks
College Bookstores: fax orders for 5+ copies to 805-899-2145

*Teacher supplements available.

This *Supplement* was prepared for use with
Sappho: The Poems, revised edition, Bandanna Books, 1993.
ISBN 0-942208-11-0

CONTENTS

THE SUPPLEMENT

Introduction

Sappho (or *Ψαπφο*, as she signed herself) was universally recognized by the ancients as the greatest lyric poet. Her lines are spare, bare, and subtle, or as Mosas Hadas put it, "it is ordinary language raised to its highest potential." Alongside the odes to Olympic athletes of Pindar, the wisdom verse of Hesiod, or the epic lays of Homer, Sappho's highly personal poems sound quite modern to our ears.

Sappho was born around 600 BC in Mytilene, the main port of Lesbos island. Lesbos is quite near Troy in Asia Minor and the major ancient trade route through the Hellespont ("bridge of the Greeks"). In fact, Agamemon, the leader of the Greeks besieging Troy, captured Lesbos himself, and noble families there, perhaps Sappho's own, traced their lineage to him.

The good harbor at Mytilene gave Lesbos economic leverage to establish trading colonies in Thrace and the Ionian coast (now Turkey). Governed by one of the Seven Sages of Greece, a dictator named Pittacus, Lesbos prospered in the century before the rise of Periclean Athens. Sappho herself boasted of the intellectual life there: "*He towers over tall men / like poets of Lesbos over all others.*"

Sappho herself was short, not known for her beauty, though Alkaios, Archilochus, and Hipponax are known to have loved her; others called her "masculine." Her father and mother, Scamandronymus and Kleis, had three sons—Charaxus, Erigyius, and Larichus—and Sappho. Her eldest brother Charaxus had an ill-fated affair with a woman named Doricha, as well as a business disaster that turned him into a vengeful pirate. Sappho married once, to Kerklyas, a rich trader from Andros, and she had one daughter, named Kleis after her mother.

For most of her life, Sappho was the leader of a school for young women, teaching poetry, music and dance based on a philosophy of love, ranging from the celebration of marriage to intimate personal feelings transformed into art. Besides poetry, her achievements include popularizing the Mixolydian mode, an emotional scale later used by Greek tragedians, and the Sapphic stanza—three lines of eleven syllables followed by a fourth shorter line. She designed a new kind of lyre, and invented the plectrum, which guitar players today rely on, the "pick."

Her work and personality evoked responses long after her death. One highly imaginative story portrays her as flinging herself over a cliff because of an infatuation with a younger man named Phaon; other stories relate that she died of old age, which I believe is more likely, based on the content of her own poems.

Late in her life, Sappho and her family, along with many noble families of Lesbos, were forced into exile for political reasons. This, too, entered her poetry. She settled in Sicily, known then as Magna Graeca because of its large Greek colonies.

Sappho's poetry was famous everywhere even in her lifetime. Three hundred years later, Plato called her the Tenth Muse. Her image was used on Mytilene coins. Though she was a prolific writer, religious intolerance in some eras sought to eradicate all her works; this slim book presents pieces gleaned from writers quoting her lines. A few additional pieces were recovered in Egypt in 1950.

This translation owes a debt to many writers who have undertaken to translate Sappho's poetry. As Edgar Lobel says, "The conjunction of extreme simplicity of language with intensity of emotion, from which the poetry derives its peculiar effect, as well as the perfection of the form, has hitherto completely baffled translators, Swinburne among the rest." This version is plain-language spoken English, and includes all of her poetry that is complete enough to be called poems; I make no attempt to imitate her rhyme schemes or Aeolian dialect rhythms.

Even the complete poems are incomplete, for the bulk of Sappho's lyric poetry was meant to be sung with musical accompaniment, and danced. Perhaps a modern-day songwriter/choreographer reading these words might bring Sappho's lyrics alive in a new way.

Sasha Newborn
July 2011

SAPPHO

THE POEMS

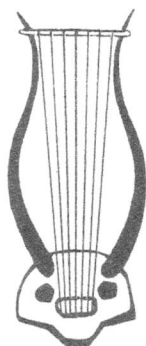

Let me tell you something:
      there will be a few who
      will remember us.

ALKAIOS: Violet-haired, pure.
honey-mouthed Sappho,
If I could speak to you,
I would say—
but shame holds me back.

SAPPHO: If you respected
goodness or truth,
your awkward words
wouldn't be forced,
shame wouldn't skulk
in your eyes
and you'd tell me
what you really want.

Ah, the sweet apple that reddens at the tip
of the branch on the topmost limb,
and which the pickers forgot—or could not reach.

Or the hyacinth on the hills that shepherds
trample unknowingly under foot, yet on the ground
the flower shows its purple.

Dika, braid your lovely hair
     with a garland
of shoots of dill
     artfully twined together:
for the Graces favor
     girls who wear flowers,
and they turn their backs
     on the bareheaded.

The folds of a purple scarf
hide your face—it was
sent from Phocaea,
for you, a cherished gift
from Timas.

Aphrodite on your shining throne,
artful daughter of Zeus,
I pray, release me
from sorrow.

Come to me, as you did once before.
You heard my voice from afar,
and, listening, left your father's
golden house

and yoked a chariot with sleek swallows
who quickly brought you from heaven
to dark earth, beating their wings
in midair.

They swiftly left; and you,
goddess, an immortal smile on your face,
ask, "What has happened now? Why do you
call me?"

"What does your mad heart crave?
What beauty would you now have me
cause to love you? Who can refuse
you, Sappho?

"No matter if she turns away, she'll soon come around,
and if now she refuses gifts, she'll soon give them,
and if she doesn't love you now, she will soon,
against her will."

Come, I pray, now, and relieve me
of this unrelenting heartache. All
that my heart longs for, may you achieve,
and be my accomplice.

If you really love me, find
a younger woman to sleep with.
I couldn't bear
to live with a man who is
younger than I am.

Since you were once an innocent child,
you can lead us sweetly in song;
apply your tongue, cry aloud your blessings for
adult pleasures.

We strut as if we were going to a wedding celebration,
so gracefully—but you walk so nervously
that our young women
could spit.

If the gods have a broad highway
to Olympus, can it possibly be available
to a human being?

Here is the dust of Timas, who,
before her wedding, was led into
Persephone's dark bedroom.
When she died far from home,
her friends with sharpened blades
snipped the curls off their heads.

No, Mika,
I won't let you.
You chose to be friendly
with the Penthil girls,
and now you treat me unkindly.

I hear a song sweetly sung by
a voice like honey,
a clear song of the nightingale
on a dewy branch.

Under a full moon rising,
the young girls stand in a circle
as if around an altar.

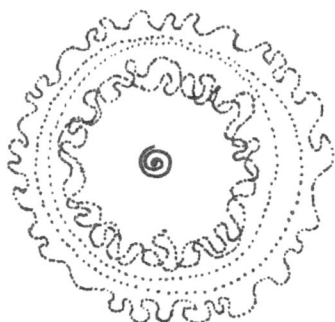

Once long ago, Cretan girls danced
in cadence around an altar of love,
trampling a ring into the soft flowering grass.

Ah, Bride, full of rose-
colored love,
brightest jewel
of Paphos,

come now
to the bedroom,
to your bed

and there
tenderly tease
your bridegroom.

May the Evening Star
lead you
bright-eyed

to the moment when
you look with awe
before the silver throne

of Hera,
queen of marriage.

Raise high the roof-beam, carpenters.
   (Here comes)
The bridegroom comes like a god,
   (the bride)
he towers over tall men
   (Sing Hymen!)
like poets of Lesbos over all others.
   (Hymenee!)

The full wine bowl already had
ambrosia mixed in,
and Hermes poured out the wine
from a leather flask for the gods.

They all clinked cups,
and poured out libations
of good luck and happiness
in honor of our new brother-in-law.

Lucky bridegroom, your wedding day has come,
and you have the bride of your hart's desire.
Her pretty face is flushed with love.

Your bride's body is shapely,
and her eyes are honeyed,
and love flows from her fair face.

Aphrodite has outdone herself
to honor you.

The doorkeeper to the bridal chamber
has feet fourteen yards long
—it takes ten cobblers to make
sandals of five hides each.

A messenger came running on powerful legs,
came swiftly to Ida with news

already known throughout the rest of Asia:
"Hektor and his men are coming home,
bringing with them a dark-eyed girl
from old Thebe on the Plakia;
gorgeous Andromache is crossing the sea
in one of our ships.

"They carry gold bracelets, and purple gowns
and strangely designed knick-knacks,
and many silver tankards and ivory scrimshaw."

So the messenger reported; astonished, Priam jumped up
and sent for his friends, and spread the news
all through the city. At once, the young men of the town
hitched the mules up to the big-wheeled carriages,

and wives and young girls crowded
inside. Priam's daughters rode together,
while youths led the carthourses
outside the city walls.

Greeting the arivals like gods, a long procession
at the seashore started back to Troy
to the noise of piercing flutes and heavy drums,
and the girls sang loudly a tuneful song
that echoed to the sky. In the streets
people offered bowls spiced with cinnamon
and jars of myrrh and incense.

Old women danced, singing the wedding march
and marching men young and old sang out
a hymn of Apollo—the great archer and lyre-player—
singing of Hektor and Andromache
as if they were gods.

Give up, groom, we'll camp outside your door
through the long night singing love songs for
you and your bride, to keep you from her violet-soft breasts.

Wake up your bachelor friends, tell them
to come. Like the nightingale, we're going to
stay awake and sing all night long.

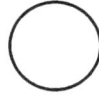

Indeed the stars anywhere near her undisguised brilliance
hold back their own shining images
wherever in the crowded sky her special brightness shines
like a silver dollar.

Lucky lady with luxuriant hair
and unfulfilled desire,
even while rumor reports that
a god is leaving you to possess another,
at the same time another fate awaits you.

Thus Aphrodite, irritated by the sirocco,
complains, with no hint of pride,
that somehow Doricha has once again
atracted a youth her own age.

The tensions of your struggle
show clearly in your face

and you could gain everything back, and more
—if it weren't for this icy numbness
of being alone.

Now, Abathis, bring a light here
to illuminate the plainly dressed Gongyla,
whose yearning soars on wings
around her beauty.

Oh, dear one, I am happy,
though once, eager and innocent, I quarreled
with Aphrodite. Now I pray
that she will soon let you go. Gongyla,
come back to me.

You came. And you did well to come.
I was waiting for you; your fire burns
my heart, it flames.

I forgive you all the endless
hours that you were away.

To me, he looks godlike,
the man who sits in front of you,
listening closely to the murmur of
your sweet words

and lovely laugh; my heart quivers
in my chest. Now, just
looking at you, I have
no voice left,

my tongue is broken, and an airy flame
runs clean through me.
I see nothing,
my ears ring,

sweat pours down me, and my body
shudders. I'm pale as dry grass, and
death seems close, familiar—
and yet

I must feel all, since I am poor.

Anaktoria—
      some prize the cavalry, while others favor
infantrymen, or the long-oared navy
as the finest sight on this black earth.
But for me, it's seeing the one you love.

It's easy to prove. Didn't Helen,
the most beautiful woman in the world,
leave her husband, the best of men, to go with
the least honorable of Trojans?

Love led her astray; she forgot
her daughter, her parents and family,
to wander light-hearted
to a distant land.

So, Anaktoria, although you are far from your friends,
don't forget us. I'd rather hear your light step
and see your bright eyes than all the glittering
chariots and armored infantry of Lydia.

Atthis—
     you said:
"Sappho, if you don't get up,
I swear, I won't love you any more.

"Get out of bed and stretch your limbs.
Pull off you Chian nightgown, and
shower like a lily by a spring.
Kleis is getting your yellow blouse and maroon
skirt from the closet. We'll put a peach-colored
cape on you, and crown you with peach blossoms.
So come on, darling, you maddening beauty!"

Love now shakes my limbs and,
pathetically,
I tremble out of control.

Yet you, Atthis, can't bear to think of me.
Instead,
you run to Andromeda.

Atthis—
       even in distant Sardis,
our dear Anaktoria must often think of us, and

of the life we shared here,
when you were a goddess to her
and your singing pleased her most deeply.

Now she glows among Lydian women like
the reddish moon after sunset blots out
the stars around her,

and spreads light equally on the salt sea
and on fields thick with flowers, with shiny dew
freshening roses and fragile thyme
and the blooming sweet clover.

She wanders everywhere, remembering
gentle Atthis, her tender heart heavy
in her breast.

She shouts aloud *Come! Come!*
We hear; a thousand ears in the night
relay her cry across the sea.

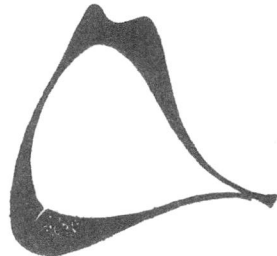

Praxinoa, honey, roast some nuts
for breakfast. One of the gods
is being good to us today—
a letter came from Atthis.

She says,

    "Sappho, the most beautiful of women,
will accompany us to Mytilene, our fair city;
she will be like a mother with all her daughters."

Dear Atthis,
have you forgotten everything?

So, I'll never see Atthis again.
Honestly, I wish I were dead.
She cried a lot when she left.
"Sappho," she said, "How can we suffer being apart?
I tell you I shouldn't go at all."

And I said,
        "Go, be happy—
just remember the one here who adores you.
And if you forget, think of all
the unsurpassed days we shared,

when we stood close together, and I
would adorn your loose hair with
violets and rosebuds and ringed your smooth neck
with twined dill and crocus;

and I'd rub your resilient skin with royal
lotion as you lay deep in the cushions of
that soft couch, while slim girls

served us everything we could desire;
and we'd be at every sacred grove,
and no chorus was chanted without us,

and the woods were filled with birdsong
as we two would wander there
together."

Leave Crete, and come to me here,
Come to your sweet apple grove and the altar
where the smoke of incense curls,

where a cold brook murmurs through the branches,
roses shade the ground, and drowsiness falls
from trembling leaves.

Sleek horses graze among the flowers and
dill is in the wind.
Here, Aphrodite, serve us gold cups of nectar
mixed neatly with pleasure.

Mermaids and brine-born Aphrodite, please
let my brother come home safely,
and allow him whatever
is in his heart.

Wash off his past wrongs,
and make him a delight to his friends but
hard on his enemies
and may he never again give cause for complaint.

May he also honor his sister,
and release me from the dark sorrow
which in other days has grieved me.

Though people justly accuse him,
may you, Aphrodite, forgive him his arrogance,
the rage to regain his name.

Sun-bleached Phoebe's and Coeus' daughter Leto
once flew as a quail with Kronos' boastful son,
Zeus of the cirrus clouds.

But her god-born daughter Artemis made
a great renunciation—

"Zeus, I swear faithfully on your very head
that I intend to remain virgin, vulnerable,
solitary and unmarried. You will see me there, on the ridge."

Then her delighted father-god spoke for all to hear:

"From now on our untamed mountain maiden
shall be called by god and human alike
by her own powerful name—Deer Hunter.
Eros is hereby relieved of approaching her."

The shining Muses and the Graces too
waited one full week before speaking her name
in the human world.

Hera, I pray you, may you
stand here gracefully beside me, as you came once
to the famous kings of Mykonos, the house of Atreus,
when they prayed.

The Atreidians won many battles
at Troy, and later on their sea voyage
home, but knew that they couldn't
come home again,

without praying to you, to Zeus,
and to Thyone's delightful son Dionysos.
Be kind, as you were before, and help me
in my own return from exile,

so that I might again be with the girls of Mytilene,
conducting the holy rites in grand style,
teaching dances and writing songs for the holy days.
Hera, bring me home.

If my womb were not finished with its work,
I might come to intimacy
atremble,

but now age and wrinkles have
caught me, and love holds back
that once chased all around my body with
tender aches.

Of all the worthy girls, it is she,
who once wore violets on her young breasts,
taking her time with me.

I regret love most of all
when it is wandering.

I have a little daughter who is like
a golden flower. Kleis, my love, I woudn't
trade you for anyone in Lydia or
in elegant Lesbos.

When our girls were young,
they used red yarn to tie back their hair;
they had no other finery.

That was enough then to be grand.
But that luxuriant hair of yours,
Yellower than torchlight, you cover with

a big floppy leaf hat
and the biggest flowers,
over a tight neat hairnet.

Now you ask me for a headband
embroidered in Persia,
or from Sardis, that elegant city.

I have no embroidered headband
for you, Kleis, and no way to get one.
In exile, such ribbons are memories.

Don't you know? As long as Mytilene
is ruled by the Kleanax family,
our name is gone.

How could I imagine
touching the sky
with my two arms?

Girlhood, girlhood, when you left me,
where did you go?
Never again will it come, never, never again.

I called you all here
to give you fine candies, girls,
and gifts, and we'll have a love song on
the pure-toned tortoise lyre.

My own skin is wrinkled now,
my black hair has gone gray,
even my knees no longer hold me up,
though I once leaped like a fawn,

but what can I do?
I can't begin again,
any more than rosy-armed Dawn
to the last days of earth can hide

her mother's love for Tithon,
whom she doomed to wither but never die.

I love this girl caressing me. I love
everything graceful. Love has given me this,
and beauty and the sunlight.

A dream on black wings
came while I slept soundly.

Its strong sorrow stole
my hope and happiness,

but I was so foolish
that games diverted me.

And I have
only this left.

Daughter, don't cry.
It's unbecoming.
Mourning should not enter
a poet's house.

Death is bad. The gods
must have thought so,
for it if were a good thing,
they then, too, would die.

Gongyla, this surely is a sign—
in a dream, Hermes came to me. I said

"Lord Hermes, you guide spirits to their final home.
I am not happy any more.
I only want to die,
and see the damp lotus
on the shore of Acheron."

SUPPLEMENT EDITION:

SAPPHO: THE POEMS

A Supplement

of critical comments

in question-and-answer format

plus Bibliography

and Glossary

BΔNDΔNNΔ BOOKS   2011   SΔNTΔ BΔRBΔRΔ

Supplement Contents

WHO WAS SAPPHO?

Sappho was a Greek speaking the Aeolian dialect (see p. 19 for Aeolian Greek), who lived mainly on Lesbos in the seventh and sixth centuries BCE. Her lyric poetry was renowned throughout the Greek-speaking world. Plato called her the Tenth Muse.

Lifespan—Cox: "We do not know with certainty the date either of her birth or of her death, but the years from 610 to 570 [BCE] may reasonably be assumed to have covered the most important part of her life."

Art showing Sappho—Sappho's likeness has been minted on coins from Mytilene and from Eresos, both with a tortoise-shell lyre on the reverse. We also know of Sappho's image from a terracotta relief from Melos in British Museum, a vase from Agrigentum, Sicily, a bust in Villa Albani (see p. 4 of this *Supplement*) that may be a copy of a bronze statue by Silanion which Cicero wrote about, a head in the Pitti Palace in Florence, a head in the Galleria Geographica in the Vatican. But there are also pieces that no longer exist: the bronze statue by Silanion, a statue in the gymnasium of Zeuxippos in Constantinople until 500 CE, a statue in Pergamon, paintings mentioned by Pliny. Several surviving pieces of art portray her with Alkaios, echoing the poem on p. 11 of the Sappho text.

WHERE DID SAPPHO LIVE?

Lesbos, then Sicily in exile, then Lesbos

Aeolian Greece—Sappho was born near the end of the 7th century BCE, and according to local tradition, her birthplace was Eresos, a city on the west coast of Lesbos south of Cape Sigrium. Lesbos was the center of Aeolian Greek culture, a prosperous fertile island rich since antiquity, situated on major trade routes. The island is 43 miles long, about 8–10 miles from the mainland (now Turkey).

Mytilene—She lived most of her life in Mytilene, the port and capital city of Lesbos. The old walls show that Mytilene was 3 miles in circumference, nearly as large as Athens.

Troy or Lesbos—Meunier: "Born in Troy according to some, in Mytilene according to others, at the end of the 6th century BCE, Sappho lived most of the time in Mytilene, magnificent capital of the island of Lesbos."

Near Lydia—Segal: "Sappho's Lesbos, well-wooded, well-cultivated and well-populated lay within several hours of Sardis, the sophisticated capital of the wealthy kingdom of Lydia."

Aeolian Migration—Powell: Lesbos was settled by Aeolian Greeks 1100-1000 BCE.

Fertile Lesbos—Cox: "Lesbos has been from the earliest ages famous for its fertility, its beauty, and the perfection of its climate....The soil is very prolific, and its oil, wine, and grain have from immemorial times been proverbially celebrated ... even as early as the Homeric poems.... Mitylene was the only Aeolian city which maintained a navy, and Lesbos had for generary generations many flourishing colonies in Asia Minor and in Thrace."

Exile—Cox: "A celebrated inscription cut in a block of marble and found at Paros ... tells us that when Aristocles ruled the Athenians Sappho fled from Lesbos to [exile in] Sicily."

WHO WAS SAPPHO'S FAMILY?

Her father's name was Scamandronymos, but he died when Sappho was just six years old. Her mother was named Kleis, who also bore three sons: Larichos, Charaxos and Eurygios.

Aristocrats—Sappho's family was aristocratic. One brother, Larichos, was a cupbearer at Mytilene, while Charaxos was a wine trader in Naukratis in the Nile delta, a Greek colony. Charaxos reportedly bought and freed a friend of Aesop's named Rhodopis, a beauty who became wealthy, while Charaxos lost his fortune. Later Rhodopis sent a gift of iron spits for sacrifices to Delphi. Sappho wrote a satirical poem rebuking her brother; we have a fragment of that poem (BB p. 36). Charaxos desperately tried to regain his fortune by questionable means in the wine trade, but tarnished his reputation in Mytilene.

Father and mother—Meunier: "Her father, from an aristocratic family, was called Scamandronymos, and her mother, Cleis."

Orphaned—Powell: "She ... was orphaned at six."

Marriage—Meunier: "According to Suidas, she married Kerkolas, a rich islander of Andros, with whom she had a daughter who, like her grandmother, had the name of Cleis. Her husband left her a widow very young."

Larichos—Meunier: "She had, it is said, three brothers. One, Larichos, served as high-ranking steward, [a cup-bearer] with the Mytilenean hierarchy, because it was the custom 'that young wellborn well-mannered men serve wine to the Mytileneans.' "

Charaxos—Meunier: "Another brother, Charaxos, became the hero of an adventure that Herodotus relates. Enriched by the wine trade and becoming enamored of the courtesan Doricha, named Rhodopis (rose-faced), who was then at Naucratis, in Egypt, Charaxos foolishly spent the greater part of his fortune and his inheritance to buy her out of bondage and set her free. To replace his ocean-going fortune, Ovid tells us that he sought 'by returning with agile ships to the blue plains, to recover his riches by dishonorable means.' Such tactics earned him, who had lost his self-esteem through an undignified love and dishonest trafficking, the bitter reproaches of his very noble sister. His towering rage didn't last long, but inexorably it turned into evil. 'If my brother failed,' Sappho sang, 'then wipe away everything, so that he does not carry any sort of dishonor to us. That he might forget the dark sadness of these occasions which he did to himself, troubles me in the heart. He can return among the dignified youths, when he can arrange for his sister to recover part of her reputation.' "

Doricha/Rhodopis immortalized—Meunier: "As for Doricha, Sappho, a woman of high race and vigilant guardian of family honor, named her an ignorant lynx, a public utility, a breath which passes. This glory of having been sung about by Sappho was always important to Doricha, [according to] the following epigram from Posidippos [translated from Thierry Sandre]: 'Doricha, for a long time you had fallen onto cinders of bones, [left with] the wheat of your hair, and your robe which carries the scent of perfumes.—Now, you have engulfed with your love the charming Charascos, and, abed near him, you have drunk profitably the breezes of morning.—Just a shining verse remains and will always remain from the dear poem which Sappho wrote to curse your name. So, your name is dignified by envy, because Naucratis will guard the memory as long as one may see boats on the Nile sail into open ocean.' "

Exile—Symonds: "Sappho spent time in exile in Sicily during her thirties, presumably as a result of her family's political activities, but later returned to Lesbos.... Her death is probably to be dated to around 570 BCE. She is reputed to have been short, dark, and ugly." Mary Patrick believes that Sappho did not marry until after returning from exile in Sicily.

Eurygios—Cox: "[A third brother is named] Eurygius, of whom, if he really existed, nothing is known."

WHAT DO WE KNOW OF SAPPHO'S POETRY?

Everything we know about Sappho is second- or third-hand.

No manuscripts—None of Sappho's original books have survived, and Sappho did not arrange her books, as far as we know. Alexandrian grammarians were the first to categorize her work into nine volumes by general subject matter. Aristophanes of Byzantium in the third century BCE prepared an edition in which the poems were arranged by poetic meter, not by subject.

Quoted—Earlier works, such as Bergk's 1914 *Anthologia Lyrica* (with 106 fragments of Sappho's poetry), garnered fragments and lines largely from quotations in the works of other writers. Curiously, Sappho proved an apt model for Greek and Roman grammarians to illustrate a number of styles and rhetorical devices.

Several new poems—Powell: "Since the 1890s ... our knowledge of Sappho's poetry has been greatly augmented by the discovery of around a hundred more fragments on papyrus ... from the sand of Egypt.... These new texts include...several substantially complete poems that easily number among her best extant works."

Archeological finds—Fragments of previously unknown poems have been found on strips of papyri in Egypt, and we may in the future find yet more.

WHAT WAS SAPPHO'S SCHOOL LIKE?

No formal school—Page: "The prestige of Wilamowitz gave new and lasting dignity to the old theory that Sappho was a paragon of moral and social virtues, and that her poetry was grossly misunderstood in antiquity. The theory alleges that she was the leader of a formal cult-association in Lesbos, devoted to the worship of an honest Aphrodite; that her companions were pupils, to whom she gave lessons on moral, social, and literary topics; that she was therefore a highly respected member of society.... The theory finds no support whatever in anything worthy of the name of fact."

Informal presentations—Page: "There is no evidence or indication that any of Sappho's poetry, apart from the Epithalamiums, was designed for presentation by herself or others (whether individuals or choirs) on a formal of ceremonial occasion, public or private. There is nothing to contradict the natural supposition that, with this one small exception, all or almost all her poems were recited by herself informally to her companions."

Personal poetry—Page: "It is clear and certain that the themes of the great majority of the extant fragments are the loves and jealousies, the pleasures and pains, of Sappho and her companions. We have found, and shall find, no trace of any formal or official or professional relationship between them: no trace of Sappho the priestess, Sappho the president of a cult association, Sappho the principal of an academy; with feigned solemnity we exorcise these melancholy modern ghosts."

Post-exile school—Meunier: "After exile, Sappho returned to Lesbos and became the leader of a group of young women, which was to earn the renown and acclamation and admiration of all antiquity. The young women whom she sought to group around her, as did her rivals Andromeda and Gorgo, were students of poetry and music. In these times so long ago, one can hardly imagine oral learning, or not being introduced to the fine arts and the disciplines of the Muses together with others in a public school, with a teacher of clarity. At Mytilene, young women who wanted to undergo training which would give them grace and beauty, united around Sappho to learn from her the complicated rhythms of Aeolian poetry, musical accompaniment and choreography. They came, some from the first families of Lesbos, others from foreign cities.... In brief, in this 'House of the Muses,' one learned everything that might prepare a virgin to become an accomplished wife, everything that would helpto develop spirit, sensibility, charm and female attraction, and to make of one's body the pure mirror of a refined soul. On Lesbos, recruitment of these 'hetairies,' on the model of religious devotees, was made much easier by the fact that the conditions of life for Aeolian women were very different from those of women in neighboring Ionia. Ionian women were restricted to women's rooms, subjected to a severe exclusion from participation in collective life, and Ionian education for women was limited strictly to the work of the hearth."

Harem to harem—Wilamowitz: "[Ionian women went] from the cage of a maternal harem to enter into one of a conjugal harem."

Aeolian inclusiveness—Meunier: "The Aeolians ... were a race enriched and bountiful, generous and ardent; the women were never excluded from any worldly relations or from liberal education."

Wilamowitz's school idea—Duban: "In discussing the social context, or setting, of Sappho's poetry, the great classical scholar Ulrich von Wilamowitz-Moellendorff early fixed—indeed, fixated upon—the idea that Sappho was a 'headmistress' running some kind of boarding school for girls ('Mädchenpensionat'). The idea, as so many of Wilamowitz's, carried the unquestioned allegiance that his name alone commanded. Though this same idea continues to surface from time to time, it has, in recent years especially, undergone increasing qualification and refinement. We may, indeed, speak of Sappho's 'circle.' But it is no longer as fashionable to speak of that circle as a *thiasos*: a quasi-religious 'college' (band, group, association etc.) devoted to the cult of Aphrodite and the Muses, with Sappho as 'priestess,' director, and chief personality binding her young devotees together with ties of intimacy and dedication."

House of Poets school—According to Mary Patrick, Sappho called her school *oikia mousopolon* (dedicated to the Muses), House of Poets.

Literary salon—Sparta and Lesbos encouraged women to organize societies for music and poetry, a practice foreign to Athens and most of Greece. Sappho's group was like a literary salon. Later societies or *thiasos* had charters which made them tax-exempt religious groups—whether Sappho's had a charter is not known. We know the names of fourteen of Sappho's students, who came mostly from Ionian mainland. She calls them *hetaerae*, which meant dedicated to the service of Aphrodite, but in later times came to mean consort.

Rival teachers—Patrick reports that Andromeda, a former student, opened a rival school in Mytilene. Another rival teacher was Gorgo. Atthis, mentioned in several of Sappho's poems (BB pp. 31–34), left Sappho's school for Andromeda's.

Writing for pay—In Patrick's account, Sappho wrote wedding-songs as a sideline, and we have a number of fragments of these. This raises the question of whether she wrote for money or not. Pindar scoffed at pay, as did Socrates, but not so the Sophists or ode writers or playwrights.

Staging—Sappho's poetry was probably written for a stage production of dancers and musicians. She no doubt heard much more poetry than she read, and probably memorized a good portion of that.

Social function—Hallett: "[Sappho had] an important social purpose and public function: that of instilling sensual awareness and sexual self-esteem and of facilitating role adjustment in young females coming of age in a sexually segregated society.... Young women could not have received sexual attentions from their suitors or hoped to find emotional gratification within marriage itself. They could only have turned to other women to become sensually aware, in order to perform adequately in the role to which their society assigned them and to find the sexual validation that could satisfy their needs. Women were the sole individuals with whom they socialized and by whom they were socialized."

WHAT WAS SAPPHO'S SEXUAL ORIENTATION?

Lover's passion—Page: "If we read Sappho without prejudice, we observe that she is deeply moved by the physical graces of young women. It is a lover's passion, not sisterly affection or maternal benevolence, which Sappho describes ... the overwhelming emotion of intensest love.... She has nothing to say about the spiritual or intellectual or moral qualities of her companions; she makes no attempt to disguise the nature and intensity of her emotions; she describes her passion again and again in words and images of uncommon force and unmistakable meaning."

Scandal is hypothetical—Symonds: "We know so very little, and that little is so confused with mythology and turbid with the scandal of the comic poets, that it is not worth while to rake up once again the old materials for hypothetical conclusions."

Middle Comedy satirists—Reinach: "You understand that during the time when the writers of [Greek] Middle Comedy, searching for characteristic types [to satirize], encountered the distant enigmatic figure of Sappho, head of a school of music and poetry, with this joy of living, this freedom of thought and of language, this disconcerting sincerity in the effusion of the most intimate emotions, they couldn't find a similar prodigy in the bourgeois society of Athens, not a single parallel case. They found, on the contrary, in the demi-monde of venal coquetry, well known examples of women who could properly speak out, but this the charming battalion was composed of interlopers, who ranged from Aspasia [an intellectual friend of Pericles, who may have written his famous Funeral oration] to Phryne [a Greek hetaera]. Not for an instant did they wonder if, by chance, women of noble families in Lesbos of the sixth century may not have lived an existence less restricted, educated more openly, with an animated role much more public than female Athenians did of the time of Plato and Demosthenes. With this lack of critical sense which characterized their age and their place, the Middle Comedy writers never hesitated to introduce Sappho in their plays as a courtesan, the very madame of courtesans. She was for them the prototype of a woman gifted with every seduction and free of all constraints, and, as they had always done throughout, in order to create laughter charged with an air of mysteriousness, they accumulated around her name every ridiculous legend and pleasant debauchery.

Sappho the legend is created—Reinach: "As a courtesan [so the Middle Comedy writers imagined], she must therefore have lovers. The poetry of Sappho, one can affirm, hardly named anyone. The imaginations of the comic playwrights were not embarrassed by so little to go on. Further, they added the famous Phaon, and all the Pleiades of old poets from one Greek island or another without regard for geography or century, from Archilochus [a hundred years early] up to Hipponax and Anacreon [a hundred years late]. They didn't forget Alkaios—the only one whose name Sappho had spoken, when he had been a compatriot, a contemporary, a fellow exile of the poetess of Mytilene—but the only one also whose verses carried the documentary proof that he had one day dared to raise his eyes to look on 'the chaste Sappho with hair full of violets, with lips of honey', the honey she was known to make by her kisses."

Socrates and Sappho—Maximus of Tyre: "Don't the works of Sappho, plus the later Maximus of Tyre (if one may be permitted to compare moderns with ancients) re-affirm all the principles of Socrates on the subject of love? Socrates and Sappho seem to me to have said the same thing, one about love between men, the other about love between women. They announce that there are numerous loves, and that beauty is always guaranteed to inflame them. What Alcibiades, Charmides and Phaedrus are for Socrates, so Gyrinne, Atthis and Anactoria are for Sappho; and if Socrates has for rivals, for certain similarities, Prodicus, Gorgias, Thrasymachus and Protagoras, Sappho has for rivals Gorgo and Andromeda. One time she gives them reproaches; another time she quarrels with them; then she takes the same ironic tone with them which is familiar from Socrates. Hail to Dion, says Socrates. A thousand things to the young Polyanacte, says Sappho. Socrates says that he no longer wishes to attach himself to Alcibiades, whom he has loved long enough, after having dressed him down appropriately by his eloquence; and Sappho says: You appear to me still a child, you are not yet formed. Socrates turns to ridicule the dress and attitudes of the sophists. Sappho speaks 'of a women in the costume of a peasant.' Diotima tells Socrates that love is not the son of Venus, but her lackey and her domestic. Sappho goes to tell Venus, in one of her odes: And you, the most beautiful of valets, Love! Diotima says again that love is radiant with health in graceful living, and that it has the pallor of death in poverty. Sappho marries these ideas in comparing sweet-sour love with bitter-sweet. Socrates treats love as a sophist; Sappho as a storyteller. The transports of love of Socrates for Phaedrus are the transports of a Bacchante; love agitates the soul of Sappho, like winds agitate the hardwoods of the mountains. Socrates reprimands Xanthippe, who cries because he is going to die. Sappho in fact says as much to her daughter: because grief should never enter into a house which nourishes the Muses; this would be against hospitality."

Ambiguous love—Duban: "Much of Sappho's surviving work is ambiguous about what type of love is at stake and is accordingly more significant than if this were clear. The love that Sappho's Aphrodite controls may be heterosexual or lesbian, and both types find expression in Sappho's work and life."

Gaiety and love—West: "Sex was for [Sappho] the private expression of a total romantic love that had its place in the context of semi-public and public gaiety and song. In this gaiety and love lay her abiding happiness."

Imaginative projection—Stigers: "Sappho's actual, personal experience in sexual relationships is not in question…[rather] Sappho's imaginative projection of emotional life into esthetically pleasing, abstract shapes."

Attraction to women—Friedrich: "Whether or not Sappho was a practicing lesbian or just passionately attracted to women is superficial compared to the more basic fact that her love must include a woman. Here lesbian love and heterosexual love are combined to contrast with male homosexuality (about which she says nothing and implies almost nothing, probably because of lack of interest)."

The circle—Bagg: "The intimacy of Sappho's circle seems to have been fervent and exclusive … the sensitive tensile threads of her personality held the [young women] in an intimacy; the [young women] felt each other through Sappho. In several poems we have a sharp picture of Sappho taking a [young woman's] emotional education in hand, showing

64

her how to read the difficult language of memory, sorrow, moonlight or sexual success and how to answer other [young women] in it. From the quality of concern in these poems we can say she created and guaranteed a community of sensibility."

The French view—Duban: "The French view of Sappho as a homosexual owes much of its popularity to the publication, in 1895, of Pierre Louÿs's *Song of Bilitis* ... [which purported to be translations of ... the autobiography of a [young peasant woman] who had belonged to Sappho's homosexual circle and later became a temple prostitute."

Ancient homosexuality—Bagg: "Homosexuality was less repressed in the ancient world than in our own age, but it would be a mistake to say that the ancients had no prejudice against consummation of this love. The sacred band was a famous oddity, and the most admired milieu where homosexual love was unashamed and cherished—the Socratic circle of Platonic love—depended for its existence on non-fulfillment of these physical desires. For Plato, male homosexual love had as its ideal a rarified, non-physical, intensely exhilarating freiendship which moved and was felt in a medium of ideas. Philosophy was its natural expression. Female homosexual love, on the other hand, lived in a medium of shared sensuality and sensibility, as Sappho shows us in her poems filled with rose chains falling on soft necks, apple boughs full of sleep, moonlit meadows, bowls full of wine, bodies full of glowing desire or harsh deprivation. Its special poignance was that this love could not fertilize the women, just as it could not engender philosophical discourse."

Loving to love—Meunier: "Loving to love, the passion of love which tormented her soul seems to have run its course without permitting her ever to meet, except in death, a place of repose from all the sorenesses from bountiful Aphrodite, all the wounds which the arrows of Eros may send to the heart. She knew and sought to speak the joys and the sorrows of loved ones present and absent, savoring and cherishing the taste and sadness of tears of voluptuousness: 'I desire and I burn with fire,' she cries! 'Eros, breaker of members, soft and bitter, insatiable and rampant, you trouble my heart, equal to the wind which sweeps through the mountains, deep over the hardwood trees!' "

Hints of pain—Meunier: "This wounded swan, who was consumed less by joy than by, as Ovid says, 'an ardor not less than the fire of Etna,' seems to have sung of distress and pain. Most of the fragments which we have remaining of her lost work hide something; they guard, like a marine conch, a discreet echo of the pains and shudders of a soul which only confided intimately to the lyre her dolorous secret."

WHAT MAKES SAPPHO'S POETRY SPECIAL?

Simple and expressive.

Many of the fragments of Sappho that we have owe their existence to her high standing among grammarians as an authority on the meanings and uses of words. She was also an exemplar of various poetic meters, including a durable one still known as sapphic (see the section on Greek poetry, p. 18). Aeolic dialect and Sappho's poetry is simple and expressive. She wrote in a time of peace, of love and friendship and loyalty.

Bursting with meaning—Thompson: "[Sappho shows] the amazing power of Greek words as words ... in such a way that phrases like ripe fruit clusters seem bursting with a rich juice of passionate meaning."

Command of resources—Cox: "She was incomparable in the perfection of every line, in the felicitous correspondence of the sense and the sound of her words, and ... she had a perfect command over all the most delicate resources of versification.... From the time of her own epoch the works of Sappho have never been entirely forgotten, and since the Renaissance the fragmentary remains of her poems have been eagerly studied by scholars of almost every country. Her meter, her style, her choice of words both as to meaning and sound, and her command of language in expressing emotion have been held up to us as exhibiting all that was most perfect in those particulars."

Nothing mediocre—Reinach: "Not a couplet, as short as might be, which did not reveal, through brusque sparks, a nature in which nothing is mediocre and a person who loves nothing in a mediocre manner; it is all the flame of the sun which shoots out very brief beams of diamond."

Elegant sweetness—Croiset: "You can divine some of the qualities of Sappho's style: the precise liveliness, the discreet realism of expression, the sparkle of images, the clarity of phrase nearly always short, perhaps an extreme softness, perhaps also vibrant and rapid. One must add to these traits those which all translation obliterates: the expressive naivete of the Lesbian dialect, the assurance of composed epithets, the sonorous freedom of rhythm. The general impression which unleashes the style of Sappho was that of an elegant sweetness, a brilliant and pure grace. Dionysus of Halicarnassus puts Sappho by the side of Anacreon and Simonides, among the masters of ornate style, flowing, agreeably melodious. This appreciation is just, but one must understand: the elegance of Sappho is not a timid elegance and for this to say negative, she does not exclude the extremes; she unites them harmoniously. She is at once gracious and forceful, naive and caressing, spiritual and passionate, but all that finely, lightly, without weighting down the details which are included in an easy and agreeable movement."

Everyday speech—Page: "Whatever else she may owe to tradition, her language is her own.... When the individual symptoms are described, the style is seen to be free from the influence of, and fundamentally different from, that of the Epic. It is realistic, severely plain and candid, unadorned by literary artifice.... Rarely, if anywhere, in archaic or classical poetry shall we find language so far independent of literary tradition, apparently so close to the speech of every day."

WHAT DID THE ANCIENTS THINK OF SAPPHO?

Exhales ardor—Plutarch: "If the son of Vulcan, if Cacus, as told by the Romans, belched forth torrents of flame and fire out of his mouth, one could well say that the words of Sappho are mixtures of flame and passion and that, in her poetry, she exhales ardor as she seethes." Or, as another translator put it, "Sappho utters words truly mingled with fire and gives vent through her song to the heat that consumes her heart."

Eloquent and soft—Demetrius: "Sappho is eloquent and soft, while she celebrates beauty, love, springtime and peace; each of these beautiful words are woven into her dream."

Homer and Sappho—Julien: "We all understand Homer to be meant when one mentions the Poet, and Sappho, when one mentions the Poetess."

No rival—Strabo: "[She was] "a marvelous prodigy.... I don't know, in all the course of time for which history has protected our memory, a single woman who has been able, throughout this great period, to rival the harvest of such lyric genius, to rival her."

Pride of Lesbos—Antipater: "A feminine Homer, and the pride of the long-tressed women of Lesbos."

What but love did Sappho teach—Ovid: "In Lesbos, what but love did Sappho teach the young women / yet Sappho's reputation was unquestionable."

Shortness—Duban: "The poem [Ovid's *Heroides* XV] contains the *locus classicus* for the idea that Sappho, in contrast to her beloved, was not especially physically graced:

> If spiteful Nature has denied me beauty's grace,
> then balance my genius in beauty's place!
> Though my size is slight, I'm famous throughout the world;
> my stature therein achieves its measurement."

WHAT WAS THE POETRY TRADITION IN LESBOS?

Strong and independent Aeolian Greek tradition

Terpander, Archilochos—Sappho's models were primarily the Lesbos poets Terpander, for his ideas combining music and poetry, and Archilochos, for his freedom in using natural, even obscene, speech and emotions in a powerful way. These two innovations allowed Sappho to create stunning, effective pieces.

Terpander—Terpander, born in Antissa on Lesbos about ninety years before Sappho, originated lyric poetry, in the form of religious songs accompanied by the cithara or lyre. His example of teaching music so influenced the Greek world that hundreds of years later Themistocles and Plato affirmed the value of musical education. Terpander's structural changes to the lyre—seven strings instead of four—made it the instrument of choice for two hundred years. He won Sparta's poetry prize at the festival of Apollo Karneia, and he may have won the Spartan prize repeatedly over a thirty-year span. Sparta's contests brought Terpander in contact with teachers and poets from all over Greece, whose ideas he introduced to Lesbos. In one poem (BB p. 21), when Sappho refers to the Lesbian poet above all others, she means Terpander.

Archilochos—Archilochos, who thrived fifty years before Sappho, was a great influence on her art, by the introduction of plain language and intimate emotions into poetry. He was a satirist, whose invective was notorious, which, when turned against his former fiancée and her father, caused a scandal. Although he traveled widely, it is said that no Greek city offered him citizenship because of his violent temper. He expanded personal poetry with his frank language and range of private emotions, he invented poetic rhythms and a dramatic presentation involving a soloist and response by a full chorus, a form which foreshadowed full-blown Greek drama. His reputation as a master of poetry was great, but in later years, many cities forbade his works because of obscenity.

Lesches—The first great poet of Lesbos was Lesches, about 700 BCE, who wrote a sequel to Homer's *Iliad*, the *Little Iliad*.

Terpander, Arion—Powell: "Sappho inherited a strong and independent poetic tradition of which she was justly proud. Though virtually nothing of Lesbian lyric poetry earlier than hers survives, we do know of two poets, Terpander of Antissa (two generations before Sappho) and Arion of Methymna (one generation before her), whose works won Lesbos a name for poetry throughout Greece."

Alkaios—Alkaios was Sappho's contemporary, an aristocratic poet of the party opposed to the democrat leader Pittakos, and not averse to using his poetry for political ends. When the aristocrats lost power, he was exiled to Egypt, but Pittakos allowed him to return years later when he was an old man. He celebrated war and drink in his poems, and was the first to write political satires, mostly against Pittakos. Critics are divided on whether the Sappho poem replying to Alkaios (BB p. 11) actually contains Alkaios' words, or whether the whole poem is Sappho's, including the rhetorical section put in the mouth of Alkaios. What do you think?

Alkman—Alkman may have been a Lydian from Sardis who ended up as a slave in Sparta. He established the function of the Greek chorus. A man of simple means, he wrote many kinds of songs in the Lesbian manner.

Stesichoros—Stesichoros was a Greek colonist in Sicily. He was born Teisias, but went by the title "choirmaster." He established the strophe, antistrophe, epode responses in poetry and dance.

WHAT WAS GREEK POETRY LIKE?

No rhyme—Barnstone: "Until very recently, it has been a uniform practice to impose rhyme on poems from ancient Greek. But the Greeks did not use end rhyme as a common poetic device."

Quantitative vs. accentual rhythms—Duban: "All classical poetry is quantitative in nature: it is the long or short quantity of each vowel that determines the length—long (two beats) or short (one beat)—of the syllable in which it appears.... In a system of this kind, the poetic stress (i.e., any 'long') is in many cases superimposed upon (and runs counter to) a word's spoken stress, or accent. Theoretically, then, two rhythms are simultaneously operative. Where poetic stress falls on an unaccented syllable, the word assumes an alternative or even a second stress."

Lyre—Lyric poetry, or poetry accompanied by the lyre, tended to be rhythmic, easy to remember. Often the lyre was simply built of a tortoise-shell with goat's horns. Sappho's lyre had five or seven strings, and she used a plectrum with the right hand, her fingers with the left. The introduction of the plectrum for stringed instruments is attributed to her.

WHAT WAS UNIQUE ABOUT THE AEOLIAN DIALECT?

Doric migration—After Homeric times (1100 BCE), the Doric migration pushed Greeks eastward, across the Aegean. The Aeolians were one of three groups of Greek peoples (the others were Ionian and Dorian) to settle on the coast of Asia Minor (currently Turkey). The Aeolic group consisted of Lesbos and twelve small towns on the coast (see map on p. 7).

Integrated meter—Powell: "Aeolic metrics envisions the poetic line not as a composite entity formed by the repetition of a given number of identical 'feet' but as an integrated whole. Nearly all Aeolic lyric verse forms have at least one choriamb (-˘˘-) at their cores; they differ in the ways that they begin and conclude. The measure which Sappho employed most frequently ... and which bears her name, the sapphic stanza, can be graphed:

$$-˘-x -˘˘- ˘——$$
$$-˘-x -˘˘- ˘——$$
$$-˘-x -˘˘- ˘——$$
$$-˘˘- -$$

where - represents a long syllable, ˘ a short syllable, and x an "anceps" syllable, one which may be either long or short."

Mode of insight—Powell: "For Sappho poetry is itself a mode of insight and a form of knowledge, [witness] the startling variety of her poems, even as they are represented among the meager remains of her nine books: poems public and personal, amorous and consolatory, intimate, ironic, and sharp-tongued, elegiac epigram, legendary narrative, marriage songs whose tones are 'popular' and 'low' beside more dignified epithalamia (and still others quietly questioning the institution of marriage), hymns of religious ritual, prayers in seeming earnest and archly poetic imitations of prayers, a propemptikon and what may be a nursery rhyme."

Smoothness—Cox: "The Aeolic dialect in which Sappho wrote is the softest, smoothest, and most direct in expression of all the varieties of the Greek language.... In it the rough breathings were absent, there was a frequent throwing back of the accent, the digamma [written as *F*, pronounced as *w*] was used to some extent."

Obscurity—Patrick: "The 'obscurity' of Sappho's Aeolic dialect in a world where Attic Greek had triumphed [helped] bring about the eventual loss of her collected poetry.... Since the 1890s, however, our knowledge of Sappho's poetry has been greatly augmented by the discovery of around a hundred more fragments on papyrus (one on a potsherd) unearthed by archaeologists from the sand of Egypt.... These new texts ... include fragments that significantly enlarge what we know of the range of Sappho's poetry."

Vernacular—Page: "The dialect of Sappho, in the great majority of the relics, is the Lesbian vernacular, uncontaminated by alien or artificial forms and features; a very small residue indicates that she wrote some poems which differed from the great majority in admitting certain features of the Epic [or Homeric] dialect.... The Aeolic ... reflects normal Lesbian usage of the time."

Fearless music—Patrick: "[The Aeolian scale and harmonies were] described as elevated and fearless."

WHAT TECHNIQUES DOES SAPPHO USE?

Sappho's poetry was used by grammarians for centuries as models for a number of poetic techniques, which she invented or popularized.

Moving caesura—Duban: "Sappho's secret consists largely in keeping her caesura (a pause in mid-verse) moving: in her sapphics the caesura seldom falls in the same place in two consecutive lines."

Polysyndeton—Segal: "The polysyndeton [many *and*s or *or*s] enhances the effect of accumulating intensity, also creates a rhythmical tempo or excitement and mounting tension analogous to the ritualizing effects of dance or drum beat."

Sapphic rhythm—Duban: "The rhythm of a Sapphic stanza consists of a thrice repeated -ᵛ -x -ᵛᵛ -ᵛ -x followed by the Epic 'tag' -ᵛᵛ -x (i.e., the line-ending cadence of all Epic poetry—Homer, Hesiod, Virgil, etc.)."

WHAT WAS LESBOS CULTURE LIKE?

Wedding songs—According to Mary Patrick, Sappho's wedding songs (*epithalamia*) were written for actual weddings. Weddings had songs at the evening banquet at the house of the bride, then the bride was taken into a chariot with more songs, and finally the wedding party moved to the new bride's house with choruses at her door or window. Other songs, or scholia (invented by Terpander), were sung by guests when the lyre was passed around.

Aeolian brilliance—Symonds: "For a certain space of time, the Aeolians occupied the very foreground of Greek literature, and blazed out with a brilliance of lyrical splendour that has never been surpassed.... Lesbos, the center of Aeolian culture, was the island of overmastering passions.... Nowhere in any age of Greek history, or in any part of Hellas, did the love of physical beauty, the sensibility to radiant scenes of nature, the consuming fervour of personal feeling, assume such grand proportions and receive so illustrious an expression as they did in Lesbos. At first this passion blossomed into the most exquisite lyrical poetry that the world has known: this was the flower-time of the Aeolians, their brief and brilliant spring. But the fruit it bore waxed bitter and rotten. Lesbos became a byword for corruption. The passions ... remained a mere furnace of sensuality, from which no expression of the divine in human life could be expected.... As soon as its freshness was exhausted, there was nothing left for Art to live on, and mere decadence to sensuality ensued."

Writing—In Sappho's lifetime writing gained common currency, first on wooden laths, then on waxed boards. Given Lesbos' education of women, it seems likely that Sappho was not only literate but well-schooled in this relatively new technique.

Social freedom—Symonds: "Several circumstances contributed to aid the development of lyric poetry in Lesbos. The customs of the Aeolians permitted more social and domestic freedom than was common in Greece. Aeolian women were not confined to the harem like Ionians, or subjected to the rigorous discipline of the Spartans. While mixing freely with male society, they were highly educated, and accustomed to express their sentiments to an extent unknown elsewhere in history—until, indeed, the present time.... The voluptuousness of Aeolian poetry is not like that of Persian or Arabian art. It is Greek in its self-restraint, proportion, tact.... All is so rhythmically and sublimely ordered in the poems of Sappho that supreme art lends solemnity and grandeur to the expression of unmitigated passion."

Beauty contests—Segal: "The women of Lesbos were famed for their beauty no less than for their sophistication. Beauty contests were a yearly occurrence."

Poetry and music—Lesbos was known as the place where poetry accompanied by music was developed best; one legend reports that Orpheus' head and his lyre drifted to the shore of Lesbos; Orpheus' music was said to have moved rocks and trees.

Nomos—The earliest known combination of poem of praise with music by flute or cithara was called the nomos, and was said to have originated in Lesbos. The nomos was a kind of chant or tone poem.

Lyre, cithara, magadis—Greek stringed instruments of this era did not have fingerboards, so that each string offered only one tone. Consequently the musical accompaniment must have been harmonically limited, though rhythms might have been complex. The larger cithara was used for public events, the lyre for home. Another variety, the magadis, was in vogue. According to Mary Patrick, Sappho is credited with inventing a stringed instrument called the Pektis, played directly with the fingers.

Prevent drunkenness—Poem reading was a common entertainment, and festivals were always musical. Common lore said that the lyre or harp could prevent gluttony and drunkenness.

Lyre as moral instrument—Patrick: "The lyre, especially, was regarded as a moral teacher, and if anyone at any time felt [oneself] losing [his/her] temper [s/he] would take up [his/her] lyre and play to calm [his/her] feelings. Not only, however, was music supposed to sharpen and improve the intellect, soften the disposition, and dissipate sadness, but it was believed that it had the power even to heal disease. Music was a method of mental and moral instruction, and helped to form the character. It was not a luxury, but a necessity."

Chorus—The Greek chorus, accompanied by flute and stringed instruments, sang for the gods before it was ever used in Greek tragedies.

Worship—Greeks everywhere looked to Delphi's Pythian oracle for guidance, also the oracle at Dodona. On the Asia Minor mainland was the ancient temple of many-breasted Diana of Ephesus. The Greeks paid homage to Dionysos and other gods, sometimes by sacrificing the best of a flock or herd, or by building beautiful temples and statues—worship through beauty.

Slavery—Some slavery existed in Lesbos, mostly non-Greek prisoners of war. Greeks on Chios, near Lesbos, were the first to buy and sell slaves from an early date. Families with slaves performing household chores freed up time for cultural pursuits, and women were then habitually educated as well as men.

Cultural centers—Lesbos was influenced by two centers of civilization: Naukratis in Egypt, which had a Greek trading settlement, and Sardis in Lydia, the court of Croesus. Sappho's own poems refer to Lydia.

PITTAKOS—PITTAKOS WAS SAPPHO'S CONTEMPORARY, A DEMOCRATIC LEADER WHO WAS ELECTED DICTATOR. HE BANISHED ARISTOCRATS, BUT ALSO MADE A GENERAL AMNESTY. HE RULED FOR TEN YEARS, THEN RETIRED. HE WAS KNOWN AS ONE OF THE SEVEN WISE MEN OF GREECE.

WHAT ROLE DID GREEK WOMEN PLAY SOCIALLY?

Women of Lesbos advanced—Cox: "There is ... evidence that in some ways the customs of the Lesbians differed from, and were in advance of, those of many of the other divisions of the Greek population. The women of Lesbos of all classes enjoyed a freedom from restraint unknown among the other Greeks."

Courtesans—Reinach: "All along, there is no example in classical Greece, and even less possible in archaic Greece, that a woman of good birth, from a thoroughly noble family, has taken the profession of the etiquette of love as her proper occupation. In the sixth century BCE, even in the most indulgent cities, the social position of courtesans remained among the most humble. Most of them were slaves."

Women's place—Reinach: "The democratic Athenians of the fifth and fourth centuries BCE only allowed a female, I mean an honest woman, a restricted and humble place in the social order. She was restricted, not despite but, because of political principles. Also all free men of the city were occupied with public and outside interests—the life of the gymnasium, of the Pnyx, of the marketplace and of the theater, more the woman, morally and materially separated from her spouse, saw herself relegated to modest works of the household and the obscure joys of the nursery. Her education was ruled by this humble destiny which for her stood as the boundaries of the city, and conversely, her destiny proved an education more and more limited in its horizon.

Freedom of courtesans—Reinach: "During the void in the social life of Athens, which sanctioned only a few educated female citizens, who were admitted openly to meetings and to banquets because they could gain men's attention through extra-marital relations or sensual pleasure, one knows that this role was filled in part by foreign women accustomed to elegant manners, luxurious jewelry, and refined culture of spirit—perhaps their many talents combined with a relaxation of moral standards.

72

I have just defined highly cultured courtesans, who never had been very numerous anywhere else."

Open society—Powell: "As a woman, Sappho had the good fortune to be born into a society which allowed her talent scope to develop, a culture which was, to judge by the evidence of her poems, markedly less misogynous and gynophobic than that of many Greek cities (Athens in particular). Women seem to have taken a large role in the social and religious life of Lesbos."

Women's room—Bascoul: "The Athenians relegated their women to the depth of the gynécée [women's room, harem], in a servitude much like Asiatic despotism. Pericles expressed the opinion of his fellow male citizens when he said that 'the best women are those who, for good or ill, create the least talk about themselves.' While their Athenian women were bored and suffering as much wounded self-esteem as if they were slaves to their bobbins and their children, their husbands went out all day, perhaps to stroll to the house of courtesans. Injustice and inequality were too flagrant, and the contrast of Spartan women who were equal to their mates was too obvious for revolt not to hatch in the hearts of female Athenians."

Clamor for women's rights—Aristotle: "There once was a time when many Athenians clamored with unthinking enthusiasm for everything Lacedemonian [Spartan]. Female Athenians saw the great prerogatives which their sex in Sparta had achieved, and they wanted to reclaim the greatest liberties, and the right to act completely at their own discretion."

Agora—The Greek agora was the town center for discussion, in which women as well as men took part.

Women poets of Lesbos—About forty years before Sappho was born, women of Sparta, Lesbos and elsewhere were writing poetry. We know the names of some of them: Myrtis and Telesilla had statues built of them, Korinna beat Pindar in some poetry contests, Cleobulina was known for riddles. Erinna, possibly a student of Sappho's, wrote an epic poem called "The Spindle"; she died at the age of nineteen.

WHAT ABOUT PARTICULAR POEMS?

BB11. ALKAIOS: VIOLET-HAIRED, PURE ...

Written by Alkaios—Page believes it is likely that the Alcaeus part was written by Alcaeus, to which Sappho replied.

Reproach—Aristotle: "They reproach what is shameful in what they speak, do, and intend, as even Sappho composed when Alcaeus said 'there's something I'd tell you etc.' ... We have no evidence one way or the other whether Alcaeus and Sappho were ever personally involved."

Chilly—Page: "Her words are certainly chilly, if not harsh and disapproving, and the metaphor ... is more colloquial than we should expect from her in such company."

Forcible metaphor—Bowra: "An unusual metaphor, and more forcible than the context requires; but not necessarily offensive of ill-humored."

Language of modesty—Mure: "Her reply is nothing more than the received commonplace of coy woman, declining a proposal which happened not to be to her taste, where the language of modesty is as habitually assumed by the loosest characters for the purposes of coquetry, as it is used in its literal sense by the most virtuous."

BB12. *Ah, the sweet apple that reddens at the tip ...*

An epithalamium—Duban: "Quoted by Syrianus in his commentary on Hermogenes. Himerius says that Sappho compared the bride to an apple, the groom to Achilles. The fragment then formed part of an epithalamium."

Avoids marriage—Gerber: "Just as the apple high up in the tree avoids being picked, so the [young woman] avoids marriage until the proper time."

Left hanging—Stigers: Because the [young woman] who values her position is hard to win she may be left hanging for want of a worthy man to pick her.... [Note the parallel of] flower and vulnerability on the one hand and fruit and inaccessibility on the other. These are two modes of coming into a relationship with men."

Catullus on the same theme —[tr. E.S. Stigers]:

"As a flower grows, hidden in a walled-off plot,
undetected by herds, uprooted by no plow,
which breezers nurture, sun and showers train
—many the boys, many the girls desiring it—
which withers when shorn by the slender blade
—and none the boys, none the girls desiring it—
so a maiden prized remains while yet untouched.
When, once defiled, she's lost her flower
boys no longer find her lovely; girls no longer dear."

Duban: "The apple is an erotic fruit both in Greek and Roman literature and is one of Aphrodite's emblems."

BB13. *Dika, braid your lovely hair...*

Garlands—Duban: "Quoted by Athenaeus. Two unsuccessfully emended verses follow which appear to indicate the Graces' preference for what is garlanded."

BB15. *Aphrodite on your shining throne...*

Brilliant—Dionysius of Halicarnassus: "The finished and brilliant style of composition...has the following characteristics: ... It would not be out of place for me to enumerate here the finest exponents of it. Among epic writers I should give the first place in this style to Hesiod, among lyrists to Sappho, with Anacreon and Simonides next to her; among tragic poets there is only one example, Euripides.... I will now give illustrations of this style, taking Sappho to represent the poets ..." [then quotes *Hymn to Aphrodite* in full; see BB p. 14]

Translations—Cox: "J.A. Symonds' rendering of the *Hymn* [to Aphrodite] ... shares with Arnold's the merit of being perhaps the best reproduction in our language of the cadence and rhythm of the original … the Sapphic meter is successfully reproduced."

Witty—Segal: "[Sappho's] dexterity and wit in evoking the love-goddess attests to her mastery of love's violence. The ritualized structure of the poem makes the mastery available and aesthetically comprehensible to others. Whatever its origins, the experience becomes a social act. It is embodied in language and song. Others can participate in it. Indeed, the mastery of love whith the poem implies—whether actual or desiderated—becomes repeatable and accessible to the poet herself on other occasions.… Needless to say, the presence of Aphrodite would not inhibit the expression of love among members of this community."

Imitation of ritual—Page: "Upon this wholly personal matter Sappho has imposed a stately and traditional form. This is not a cult-song.… This poem is, in form, an imitation of that type of ritual-prayer which is rather a demand for a particular service than a general act of worship; the pattern of such prayers is immemorially old.… A peculiar feature of the poem is the relatively long discription of the descent of Aphrodite from heaven on some previous occasion. Here superstition and art go hand in hand.… Sparrows were sacred to Aphrodite, symbolic of her powers.… It is evident, here and elsewhere, that the talent which enables her thus to describe and criticize her deepest emotions dispassionately, allows her also to remember that she will be reciting her verses for the entertainment of her friends.… Here, at the height of her suffering, she devotes a quarter of her poem to such a flight of fancy, with much detail irrelevant to her present theme."

BB21–28. *Wedding songs, or Epithalamia*

Epithalamia—Page: "It is appropriate here to make two general observations: first, that all the fragments of Sappho hitherto classed as abnormal in dialect are or may be hymeneal in character; secondly, that the Epithalamia are (with one exception) the only poems of Sappho which might be described as ceremonial.… It seems probable that there is some necessary connexion between these facts; but, if so, its nature is problematic.… Hymeneal songs were sung at different stages of the wedding ceremony: at the banquet; during the preocession to the bridegroom's house, outside the closed and guarded bridal chamber in the evening, and again the next morning."

BB22. *Raise high the roof-beam, carpenters* …

Some readers will recognize the source of J.D. Salinger's story title here.

Hymen—Hymen is reputed to be the god of marriage, traditionally greeted in the hymeneal song at the wedding ceremony.

Better spoken than sung—Demetrius: "The style in which [Sappho] mocks the awkward bridegroom or the keeper of the wedding door is very different. It is quite commonplace, and the words are better suited to prose than to poetry. Indeed, these poems of hers can be better spoken than sung, and would not be suitable for the chorus or the lyre, unless for a kind of talking chorus."

Playful—Bowra: "This is neither bawdy nor exalted, but playful. If the humor is a bit primitive, that is due to tradition, which expected jokes at this level."

Ithyphallic—Gerber: "If Kirk is right in his explanation that the bridegroom is so described 'because he is fantastically ithyphallic' (hence the order to raise the roof), this is the only example in Sappho of the ritual obscenity common in wedding-songs."

BB23. *The full wine bowl already had ...*

Quoted by Athenaeus.

BB24. *Lucky bridegroom, your wedding day has come ...*

Quoted by Hephaistion.

BB25. *The doorkeeper to the bridal chamber has feet ...*

A rescue attempt—Traditionally, the bride's friends would mount a "rescue" after the newlyweds had entered the bridal chamber, but the door would be guarded by at least one friend of the groom, here the butt of a burlesque joke.

Risqué jokes—Duban: "Risqué abuse was a common feature of Greek wedding songs."

BB26. *A messenger came running on powerful legs ...*

Not Homeric—Page: "Although she borrows freely from the dialect and vocabulary of Homer, she is not at all concerned to portray a Homeric scene. There is indeed no Epic model for the celebrations which she describes; her portrait is drawn ... from contemporary life.... The language is traditional; the story is her own design."

Delirious passion—Longinus: For instance, Sappho everywhere chooses the emotions that attend delirious passion from its accompaniments in actual life. Wherein does she demonstrate her supreme excellence? In the skill with which she selects and binds together the most striking and vehement circumstances of passion.... Are you not amazed how at one instant she summons, as though they were all alien from herself and dispersed, soul, body, ears, tongue, eyes, color? Uniting contradictions, she is, at one and the same time, hot and cold, in her senses and out of her mind, for she is either terrified or at the point of death. The effect desired is taht not one passion only should be seen, but a concourse of passions. All such things occur in the case of lovers, but it is, as I said, the selection of the most striking of them and their combination into a single whole that has produced the singular excellence of the passage."

Narrative poem—Duban: "Preserved on papyrus. The poem differs from most of Sappho's ... poetry in being narrative, instead of highly personal, and in exhibiting throughout the characteristics of Epic dialect, meter and style.... Homer nowhere depicts the marriage of Hector and Andromache.... The theme, a well known part of the Epic tradition, is one to which Sappho brings her own distinctive emphases and flavor. Some of these are bitterly ironic.... The wedding couple's entrance (in a cart accompanied by shouts) bears [similarity] to the entrance of Hector's ransomed corpse in the last book of the Iliad. Sappho's wedding poem comes close to being a funeral dirge in disguise."

A quibble—Most translators identify Idaeus as the messenger's name; I identify it as Mount Ida, southeast of Troy.

BB28. *Give up groom, we'll camp outside your door ...*

From the same papyrus as BB30.

BB29. *Indeed the stars anywhere near her undisguised brilliance ...*

Quoted by Eustathius.

Moon rhythms—E. Stigers: "[The poem connects women with] the mysterious rhythms of the moon as separate from the sharp, bright male world of sun and stars."

BB32. *You came. And you did well to come....*

Quoted by Julian; attributed to Sappho.

BB33. *To me he looks godlike ...*

Catullus's version—Duban: "Catullus' version of the poem [Poem 51, translated freely] has a fifth stanza on the ruinous consequences of sloth (*otium*). Beyond the note of shared self-admonition, the stanza would appear to diverge completely from its Sapphic predecessor."

Hall's translation—J. Hall (seventeenth century translator of Longinus, which included Sappho's *Ode*, died at thirty-one):

> He that sits next to thee now and hears
> Thy charming voyce, to me appears
> Beauteous as any Deity
>   That rules the skie.
> How did his pleasing glances dart
> Sweet languors to my ravish'd heart
> At the first sight though so prevailed
>   That my voyce fail'd.
> I'me speechless, feavrish, fires assail
> My fainting flesh, my sight doth fail
> Whilst to my restless mind my ears
>   Still hum new fears.
> Cold sweats and tremblings so invade
> That like a wither'd flower I fade
> So that my life being almost lost,
>   I seem a Ghost.
> Yet since I'me wretched must I dare."

Stiff translation—Cox: "[Hall's translation is] stiff and without distinction."

Interested bystander—Page: "Sappho speaks of her sensations as dispassionately as if she were an interested bystander."

Congress of emotions—pseudo-Longinus (tr. Hamilton Fyfe): "Is it not wonderful how she summons at the same time soul, body, hearing, tongue, sight, colour, all as though they had wandered off apart from herself? She feels contradictory sensations, freezes and burns, thinks unreasonably.... She wants to display not a single emotion, but a whole congress of emotions. Lovers all show such symptoms as these, but what gives supreme merit to her art is, as I said, the skill with which she chooses the most striking and combines them into a single whole."

Uncommon objectivity—Page: "[Sappho here exhibits] uncommon objectivity of her demeanour toward her own extremity of passion; the accurate definition of its physical symptoms; the rare gift of vivid, brief, and precise expression. These thoughts could hardly be put into words more candid, apt, and luminous."

Loves the young woman—Page: "[The man] disappears from sight at the end of the first stanza.... Sappho loves the [young woman]: and it is clearly suggested that the [young woman] is not, at least at this moment, particularly interested in Sappho.... Two only among her symptoms have no counterpart in Homer: the subtle fire that steals under the flesh, and the humming in the ears; it is to be observed that neither of these recurs in later poetry."

At a wedding—Wilamowitz: "The poem describes Sappho's emotions at seeing, perhaps for the last time, a beloved pupil who is leaving her for a husband."

Not a wedding song—Page: "[Wilamowitz, Snell, and Bowra separately offer] a modern misinterpretation of the poem ... that it was sung at a wedding ceremony, where Sappho is assisting at the marriage of a favourite 'pupil.' The man in the first stanza is 'the bridegroom.'... The truth is that [their] theory was based on nothing but a preconceived notion about Sappho's moral character: the search for confirmatory evidence came later, and proved utterly vain.... The ancients, who knew this poem in its completeness, had no doubt about its meaning. To Longinus, to Catullus, to Plutarch, it was a masterpiece among poems of passionate love."

An illusion—Lefkowitz: It is important to remember that what she is describing is an illusion, 'he seems to me,' 'I seem to myself.' ... The time is indefinite, the illusion happens over and over: 'whenever I look at you.'...The man has no specific identity; he is 'whoever ... sits opposite.' The exaggerated terms in which the narrator's reactions are described add to the sense of illusion: the broken tongue, the sweat that grasps, the shuddering ... and being greener than grass do not portray the condition of the narrator in real life.... What the man has that she doesn't have ... his physical strength; he seems 'like the gods' while she is faint and powerless."

BB34. *ANAKTORIA—SOME PRIZE THE CAVALRY, WHILE OTHERS FAVOR ...*

The setting—Menelaus was the husband of Helen, whom she left for Paris, son of King Priam of Troy. Her daughters were Hermione and Megapenthes, and her home had been Sparta.

Feminine ideal—Duban: "The poem is preserved on papyrus. Sappho sees her own feminine ideal against the masculine ideal of such as delight in a military display."

Most beautiful—Stigers: "[This poem describes Helen] as the most beautiful and as making the choice about what is most beautiful."

Story of Helen—Bowra: "The story of Helen is not ... a warning, but an example, readily understood, of the power of love to break familiar bonds and force its victims to risk everything for it. Sappho makes it the center of her life, because it is not only radiant and enthralling but in the end irresistible."

Repeated comparisons—Page: "The conventional comparisons with which the poem began are now repeated, but with a difference: here they stand in contrast not with a general sentiment but with those particular qualities of the beloved which move the heart of Sappho to ecstasy—the way she walks, and the bright sparkle of her face."

The favorite's name—Page: "From the moment when Sappho says 'the object of your love,' the audience will be alert to catch the name of the favourite. Sappho keeps them in suspense for a moment."

War-chariot—Lorimer: "Sappho still knows of the war-chariot, but only as Lydian ... and perhaps only as a romantic appendage of bygone warfare."

BB36. *Love now shakes my limbs and ...*

Andromeda—Quoted by Hephaistion, who elsewhere quotes "Andromeda [Sappho's rival] has her just deserts."

Turmoil—Bowra: "In a very few words Sappho conveys the turmoil of her state which is both physical and mental and which she both welcomes and hates."

BB37. *Atthis—Even in distant Sardis ...*

This poem is from same parchment as BB 39.

Absence—Duban: "Both [BB37 and BB39] are poems of departure or absence. Sappho comforts Atthis by assuring her that another [young woman], now in Lydia, has not forgotten her. The greater part of the poem is occupied by Sappho's most expansive surviving simile. The poem begins after three broken lines and trails off into 19 highly fragmentary lines."

Simple theme—Page: "So simple is the theme, and it is doubtful whether there are more subtle undertones to be detected.... The description of the moonlight does indeed indicate that Sappho's thought passes from the imaginary to the real: her moon begins as a symbol for the [young woman]'s beauty, and ends as a real moon.... Finally the symbolism is forgotten, the illustration becomes a digression, and the return to the principal theme appears abrupt."

Reddish moon—Friedrich: "[This is] an extradorinary symbol that combines a reddish dusk, a transformation of a setting sun into a rising moon, an erotic condensation of Lesbian love play, and perhaps, an experiment with a new, woman's language."

Extended simile—Page: "[The simile] has gone so far beyond its starting point that the [young woman] is, for the moment, forgotten. [Note] the principal attempts, all unsuccessful, to define a delicate relationship between the simile and the theme, between the description of the natural functions of the moon and the consolation of Atthis or the beauty of the absent [young woman]."

The moon—Bagg: "The moon is both a mental image of comparison and a sight to behold; and the longed-for [young woman]'s essence flows easily from the one into the other.... Her beauty and far-off-ness and presence are implicitly emanating from the moon. ...Their friend's personality is spreading toward them through the medium of moonlight, encourages the dew to make flowers blossom and will have a reviving effect upon Atthis."

BB39. *So, I'll never see Atthis again ...*

Sixth century—Duban: "Preserved on a sixth century parchment... the same parchment contains ... several other scraps."

Shared memories—Stigers: "The poem preserves the moment when Sappho transmutes the old, physical closeness into a new purely emotional connection. So the poem becomes the container of shared memories, hence itself the privace space ... either can enter and find the other imaginatively."

Wish to die—McEvilley: "The wish to die, as often in Sappho, is a metaphor for the rejection of present time, and memory, that tomb where the present lies when it has died, may serve as a surrogate for physical death."

Delicate contrast—Page: "The inner meaning, and the mood reflected, are more elusive. It appears, first, that Sappho deliberately contrasts her own behaviour with that of her companion. She is, if not resigned, at least self-controlled.... Her companion, on the other hand, is weeping and in despair.... But now there is evidently a further and more delicate contrast—between the self-possession and strength of character which Sappho displayed at the time of parting, and the despair which she confesses now, when she reflects upon it.... And so there follows a further consequence. Her words of comfort, her reminiscences of past delights, served the purpose at the time of consoling her companion: but what purpose do they serve now? ... The words which she spoke then to relieve her companion's sorrow she must repeat now to relieve her own."

Conventional or personal—Page: "It still remains to inquire whether the portrait is personal or conventional.... It seems conventional enough, no more applicable to the departing [young woman] than to any other member of the society. There is nothing profound in the expression, though there may have been much that was poignant in the emotion."

Sorrow—Wilamowitz: "[Sappho uses here] words of sheer and absolute sorrow."

BB40. *Leave Crete, and come to me here ...*

On pottery—Duban: "Written on a potsherd in a hand assigned to the third century BCE, and therefore one of the two oldest surviving remnants of the text of Sappho. The only lyric fragment thus preserved. Parts of this poem were quoted by Hermogenes and Athenaeus."

Corrupt text—Page: "There is no distinction between lines in the stanza; at the ends of the stanzas themselves a small space is left vacant. The text is remarkably corrupt, though the hand is surely a fluent and practiced one; the writer was either very careless or very ignorant, or both."

First part missing—Page: "It is ... unlikely that the stanza beginning [the poem here] was the first of the poem."

Hallucination or conventional—Page: "We have the choice between two inferences, and shall choose the second: either Sappho suffered from chronic hallucinations, or her experiences of epiphany are conventional, in the sense that while she shared the popular belief that divinities might intervene on earth in answer to invocation, she did not suppose that she regularly saw them in human guise. That is not to say that epiphanies in Sappho are nothing but poetical motifs: she might have no visible proof, but she could have faith; there is no reason to suppose that she did not hold the accepted opinion of her own and later generations. The question then arises whether Sappho's prayers ... were devotional ... or literary and personal.... It is surely obvious that the latter alternative is correct.... It is obvious that such poems are, first and foremost, records of personal experience, designed to be heard rather by mortals than by gods."

Not fictitious—Page: "Nor must we too hastily assume that Sappho's conversations with the gods are purely fictitious."

BB41. *Mermaids and brine-born Aphrodite, please ...*

Charaxos and Rhodopis—Herodotus: "Rhodopis was in her heyday during the reign of Amasis.... She was a Thracian by birth, slave to Iadmon.... Rhodopis arrived in Egypt ... to ply her trade, but was redeemed at a high price by ... Charaxus ... brother of Sappho the poet.... Rhodopis, thus liberated, remained in Egypt; and such were her fascinations that she made a great fortune ... but not sufficient for the building of such a pyramid [The pyramid of Mycerinus was popularly called the work of "Rhodopis the courtesan"].... When Charaxus returned to Mitylene after liberating Rhodopis, Sappho taunted him severely in a poem."

Doricha—Page: "Strabo notices that Herodotus' 'Rhodopis' is called 'Doricha' by Sappho.... Athenaeus says that Doricha herself had a share of hard words in Sappho's verse."

Not a complete poem—Page: "It is evident that the present fragments do not represent the poem to which Herodotus alludes. For he says that she mocked or taunted her brother."

Unfair to Charaxos—Page: "[Charaxos] was indeed unfortunate. His sister spread the tale of his indiscretions, in memorable form, throughout his native island; and then, when he showed some natural annoyance, carried on her side of a domestic quarrel in widely circulated verses to which he may well have been unable to make an adequate reply. If we are trying to read the character of Sappho, we must not ignore what we find written here. Modern sentiment has drawn a very different conclusion from the poems."

Voice of reproach—Smyth: "Sappho's sensitiveness to the voice of public reproach occasioned by her brother's ill-fame is morally inconceivable had she herself not been innocent of the turpitude with which she was charged by the Athenian writers of comedy."

Disapproval—Bowra: "True to her aristocratic upbringing, Sappho disapproved strongly of Charaxus' quixotic action towards a woman outside her own society, and there could be no better evidence for Sappho's own high standards of conduct."

Notoriety—Page: "It was not the fact but the extravagance of the liaison which aroused her fury.... The waste of money was bad enough; and it is likely that the notoriety of the affair caused Sappho much vexation at home and in the city. It appears that she was prepared to forgive and forget; but when her brother declined the proffered reconciliation, she used the weapon which lay ready to her hand...There is nothing unnatural in her conduct ... above all there is nothing to indicate the presence of superior virtues in herself."

BB43. *Hera, I pray you, may you ...*

Odyssey account—Page: "In the third book of the *Odyssey* Nestor tells the story of a quarrel between the sons of Atreus. ...Nestor and his company sailed to Lesbos, whither Menelaos later followed them. At Lesbos they stayed to take thought about their further voyage, and prayed to Zeus for a sign.... He told them to choose the passage straight across the Aegean to Euboea. The text of Sappho proves that the Lesbian version of this story differed in certain important details.... Agamemnon was present beside Menelaos in Lesbos, whereas according to the Odyssey the two had parted company long ago. Sappho's version either told nothing of the quarrel, or supposed a reconciliation...Further, the Atridae in Sappho's poem pray not to Zeus only, as in the Odyssey, but to the peculiar Lesbian trinity of Zeus, Hera, and Dionysus.... Thirdly, whereas in the Odyssey the Achaeans pray only for guidance in the choice of a passage to Hellas ... in Sappho's poem their difficulties are perhaps greater.... There was something which they 'could not do' until they implored the favour of the trinity.... The theme of this poem ... was probably some personal matter, to which the allusion to the Atridae was subsidiary."

BB45. *I have a little daughter who is like ...*

Quoted by Hephaistion.

Agapata—J. Hallett: "For the first time on Greek literary record, we find an adjective [*Kleis agapata*: beloved Kleis] previously used only for male children ... applied to a daughter. [*Agapata* is] a word for someone prized in a non-sexual way, specifically a parent's, or sole guardian's sole offspring."

BB46. *When our girls were young ...*

Oldest papyrus—Page: "By far the oldest extant papyrus of Sappho or Alcaeus." Last half of poem is fragmentary.

BB48. *Girlhood, girlhood, when you left me ...*

Quoted by Demetrius.

BB46. GONGYLA, THIS IS SURELY A SIGN— ...

On papyrus—Duban: "Preserved on papyrus as vs. 11-14 of a sixteen verse fragment.

Switches epic motifs—Boedeker: "Sappho clearly recalls well-known epic motifs concerning death and the afterlife, and then reverses her audience's expectations.... The narrator refuses the offer of Hermes, desires rather than fears a transition to the world of death, and imagines a Hades of fertility and tranquility. The poem becomes a new, personal statement of values, a denial and reshaping of epic-heroic ideals. The end result is one that only she could envision: a death that nurtures, an Elysian Acheron.... Lotus, first, implies the fertile beauty of flowers and the easy nurture of fruit effortlessly gathered.... The lethe induced by the Odyssean lotus may well have influenced Sappho's choice of plant in this setting: not only is her Acheron floral and fertile, perhaps it also nurtures oblivion to the cares which motivate the desire for death."

Gongyla—Page: "Gongyla, who came from Colophon, was already known as one of Sappho's companions."

WHAT IS THE CONTROVERSY ABOUT SAPPHO?

Position of Sappho—Reinach: "If the critics of all times have unanimously celebrated the poetic gifts of Sappho—the exquisite choice of words, the natural and audacious turn of thought, the grace of images, the supple magic of rhythms—on the other hand, differing opinions have existed since antiquity on the social position and moral value of Woman. Should she be a courtesan or a grand dame? Can one see in her this high and pure figure of the impassioned Muse, that Plutarch compared to Pythias on his tripod, or a vulgar lover and I don't know what sort of professor of depravity?"

No evidence of low standards—Cox: "However the question may be considered, there is no trustworthy evidence to prove that, at the time when Sappho lived, the moral standards in Lesbian society were low."

Two Sapphos—Reinach: "Thus were created all those pieces by the fantasy of the comic writers, accepted without objection through these superficial anecdotes which were related by Hermesianax and Chameleon, and much later by the Fathers of the Church. The figure of the courtesan Sappho was so well taken bodily into literary history that the erudite Alexandrians, despite their alert critical spirit, did not dare to repudiate the characterization entirely. Moreover, the contrast between the outraged madwoman who ends as an amorous grisette and the noble poet whom, says Aristotle, the Mytilenians honored as a heroine, is striking. The quandary of grammarians was extreme. Some resolved the affair by distinguishing between two Sapphos: the hetaera of Eresos, whom the comic writers had written about in their plays, and the Muse of Mytilene, whose poetry was read by everyone. Other critics contented themselves by posing, without resolving, the question: An Sappho publica fuerit [Will Sappho have been open to the people]?"

Amateurs of scandal—Meunier: "Modern erudition has inherited these contradictory traditions and these perplexities, with this disadvantage, that it lacks, in order to decide, one essential document in the dossier: the complete collection of Sappho's poems. Failing this, one counts on authorities; and since, among the sweepers-up of crumbs of history, the amateurs of scandals have always been the majority, one need not be astonished if, most often, the balance swings to the worse side."

Pros and cons—Meunier reports that Welcker and Otto Muller support Sappho's good reputation, while the Englishman Mure speaks against it.

Reputation—Croiset: "[In Sappho's case,] it is always necessary to guard against associating words with acts, and of certain habits of style with habits of conduct."

WHO OPPOSED SAPPHO AND WHY?

Against women—Meunier: "To put a halt to such pretensions, the comic writers parodied the works of Sappho, and calumniated her, to depreciate and vilify the women and to cut short their revindications, the most noble and the most famous of all those in whom genius seemed to authorize their rights to a just revolt."

Phaon from Ovid—Cox: "T[homas] W[entworth] Higginson ... repudiates the calumnies of the comic writers of later centuries, such as Ameipsias, Emphis, Antiphanes, Diphilus, Ephippus, and Timocles ... and he traces the Phaon legend to its Ovidian source. He mentions Welcker's important essay published in 1816 ... a successful effort to clear away the obloquy [and] scandal."

Decadence—Cox: "Beginning two or three centuries after the death of Sappho there was a gradual development of a certain amount of obloquy in connection with her name ... until, leaving her genius out of the question, her name came, to some extent, to connote decadence and depravity.... The first important disseminators of the scandal were the later comic writers who apparently attacked her reputation in the same way in which, by the use of satire and suggestive allusion, they attacked other famous individuals. They used Sappho merely as a celebrity whom they considered vulnerable... From an evidential point of view these onslaughts may be safely disregarded."

Medieval attacks—Cox: "Later, during the Middle Ages, Sappho seems to have suffered attack ... because she, like other lyric poets, wrote what some austere fanatics chose to consider frivolous and, according to their views, immoral poems. The attacks of this nature were against her works rather than against her character.... Many other ancient writers were treated in the same way."

Assaults on poetry—Cox: "Among the writers singled out for ... assaults of bigotry and destructiveness were the ancient lyric poets, and it is a matter of knowledge that among these Sappho was a prominent victim. There is known to have been one orgy of such destructiveness about [CE] 380 at the instigation of Gregory Nazianzen, and another in the year 1073 when Gregory VII was pope. Rome and Constantinople were the chief centers of this madness."

Athenian attackers—Two hundred years after her death, at least six

84

Athenian writers, including the playwright Menander, slandered Sappho's reputation, attributing a loose lifestyle to her on the basis of her poems.

Early Christian attackers—380 CE Sappho's books were burned in Constantinople, and by Justinian in the 6th century. Also 1073 under Pope Gregory VII.

DID SAPPHO LEAP FOR LOVE?

Unsinkable legend—An unsinkable legend about Sappho is that she plunged down a cliff in Leukadia near Ithaca out of unrequited love for a younger man, Phaon. The Leukadian rock is a vertical rock 2,000 feet above the sea, fabled for the "Leukadian Leap," an annual sacrifice to Apollo. Also, Sappho is known to have written several songs about a legend of Phaon, an old man who had been transformed by Aphrodite into a beautiful young man who was, however, indifferent to love. Edwin Arnold and a number of modern critics reject the Phaon legend, a favorite story through the Middle Ages and revived in the nineteenth century.

Allegory—Cox: "The [Phaon] story is no doubt a myth founded on an allegory tricked out in the meretricious trappings of mediocre poetical efforts.... Modern English writers justly treat this Phaon legend as incredible."

Strabo's account—Duban: "Strabo ... notes an old custom of the Leucadians every year at the sacrifice of Apollo (whose temple was atop the cliff). As an apotropaic, or averting, rite, they would throw some guilty person from the cliff. Flapping birds and feathers were attached to the victim to break the fall, and a large crowd waited in boats below to rescue him [or her] and, if possible, carry [her or] him to safety beyond the frontier.... Curiously, by Servius' time (again some 500 years later) we find an attentuated version of the ritual. Servius, while leaving the purpose of the leap unspecified, speaks of the custom 'now in vogue' of hiring people once a year to throw themselves from the cliff into the sea. The notion of hire would seem to indicate little more than some form of entertainment."

Roman retelling—Menander: "[Sappho] first leapt from the far-seen rock in wild love-chase of the proud Phaon."

Ritual poetry—Kirkwood: "[The Sappho-Phaon story] probably took its rise from the fact that Sappho wrote poetry to be used at a ritual honoring a year-spirit either identical with or like Phaon.... [It became legend] arising most likely from Sappho's poetry, expanded by comic burlesque in the fourth century, and perpetuated by Ovid."

WHOM DID SAPPHO INFLUENCE?

Roman revival—Cox: "In the time of Augustus there occurred the first revival of Roman interest in her works.... Catullus was the foremost ... and he was more successful than any of his Roman contemporaries in entering into the spirit of the Greek rhythm. Horace also was a successful imitator of the Sapphic meter.... Ovid's epistle, 'Sappho to Phaon,' belongs to this period, but whatever may be its poetical and literary merits, it may, from a historical and biographical point of view, be safely disregarded."

Alexandrian scholars—Powell: "Two of the great scholars of Alexandria in the third and second centuries BCE, Aristophanes of Byzantium and Aristarchus of Samothrace, collected and edited her poems in nine books arranged according to meter. The first of them (poems in the sapphic stanza) contained 1,320 verses, though others were probably shorter; nevertheless, it is apparent that originally the corpus of her poetry was fairly substantial." What we have now, including fragments, amounts to about 500 lines.

Latin lyric—Powell: "In the first century BCE, [Sappho's poetry] exercised a seminal influence on the flowering of the Latin lyric. Catullus translated what is probably her best-known poem ['To me he looks god-like,' BB p. 28] and adopted its sapphic stanza in one of his own most successful lyrics, and the example of her architectonics and psychology was crucial to Horace in his Odes."

Roman poets—Catullus revived her reputation in Augustan times, and Ovid and Horace imitated her songs.

WHAT DID LATER CRITICS SAY?

Beautiful fragments—Joseph Addison: "Among the mutilated poets of antiquity there is none whose fragments are so beautiful as those of Sappho." Addison's comments in 1711 stimulated interest in Sappho, and several translations appeared subsequently.

Exquisite—Edwin Arnold: "[Sappho is an] exquisite poetess ... whose genius among all feminine votaries of singing stands incontestably highest ... the purest impersonation of the art of lyric song." Arnold rejected the Phaon legend.

Every word a perfume—John Addington Symonds: "Of all the poets of the world, of all the illustrious artists of all literatures, Sappho is the one whose every word has a peculiar and unmistakable perfume, a seal of absolute perfection and illimitable grace."

Poetry as insight—Jim Powell: "This variety [is not] the result merely of a taste for generic diversity, of stylistic motives. This can be seen in the paradoxical fact that a careful, sensitive, plainly literal prose translation will convey a great deal of Sappho's intensity ... so much of the power of Sappho's poetry is wrapped up in what it says."

Psychology—Powell: "The melodic intensity and incandescent emotion of Sappho's poetry are often praised; her psychological penetration and irony are less widely recognized. Unlike the verbal irony of Propertius (or of most modern poetry), Sappho's is much more dramatic than linguistic—structural and situational more than verbal. It appears when we reflect on what she is telling us, and what she isn't, on the difference between what a poem says and what it implies about the one who says it. Sappho may trigger our reflections with a pointedly chosen word: but she prepares them in the action of her poems, in their narration. Sappho employs irony not for its own sake or to maintain a safe distance between herself and her subjects but as a means of revealing contradiction, a way of staging it.... Sappho is interested in ironic dissonance not for the poetic frisson [thrill] it produces but as a means of opening the doors of perception.... Like her poetry itself, they are a mode of insight."

Literate lyric—Powell: "With some show of reason Sappho may be said to have invented the literate lyric for western literature, and as an artist she is without doubt our contemporary, but as a stylist, not remotely. Many of her poems imitate the tones of intimate, natural speech, but many others engage and play off conventions of diction and rhetoric far from conversational norms."

Uneven work—Page: "The modern estimate of Sappho as a lyrical poet of the highest order must still be founded, as heretofore, on two poems, *Hymn to Aphrodite* [BB p. 14] and *He seems godlike* [BB p. 28].... Much of her poetry was below the standard by which we were accustomed to judge her. It is questionable whether there is anything among the new fragments which reaches or even approaches the level of the old. We discern in both old and new the same narrow limitation of interests, the same simplicity of thought, the same delicacy in expression, the same talent for self-detachment and self-criticism."

Very greatest poet—Algernon Charles Swinburne: "Judging even from the mutilated fragments fallen within our reach from the broken altar of her sacrifice of song, I for one have always agreed with all grecian tradition in thinking Sappho to be beyond all question and comparison the very greatest poet that ever lived. Aeschylus is the greatest poet who ever was also a prophet; Shakespeare is the greatest dramatist who ever was also a poet; but Sappho is simply nothing less—as she is certainly nothing more—than the greatest poet who ever was at all. Such at least is the simple and sincere profession of my lifelong faith."

WHAT PROBLEMS IN TRANSLATING SAPPHO?

Quantitative—Duban: "Ancient Greek poetry is quantitative: it creates its rhythms by organizing the succession of longer and shorter syllables, rather than of syllables more and less stressed, as English does."

Loose translations—Duban: "It is ... precisely the absence from Greek poetry of rhyme and meter as we know it that is responsible for the pervasive freedom of form and content in translation today.... Despite frequent avowals to the contrary, there is no way that the essential features of Greek poetry—a quantitative (as opposed to accentual) meter, a highly inflected, polysyllabic, vowel-rich vocabulary, a broadly flexible word-order—can be rendered into English or any language."

Lattimore's translation—Duban: "[Richmond] Lattimore ... precisely reproduces the syllabilification, and to large extent, rhythm of the original.... The poem overall, attractive. Inasmuch as Lattimore's is a superior rendering, it is regrettable that he chose to keep his work within the strictest confines of a 'selection.' He translates only nine pieces by Sappho."

Inaccuracy of rhyme—Madame Dacier: "Les traductions en vers sont peu fidèles" [Translations into rhyme are not very accurate].

English not unsuitable—Cox: "Some writers ... emphasize the disadvantages of English as a language into which to translate Greek poetry.... It is not really that English is an unsuitable or inferior language for the expression of poetic conceptions, but that it is different, and that the transfer of perfection in one language into perfection in another is not within the bounds of possibility. Approximation is all that even genius can hope for in the attempt."

Sparrows, for instance—Cox: "The translation of *strogthoi* by 'sparrows' does not seem a very happy one in spite of its use by Symonds and some others. It is true that *strogthos* means a sparrow or a small bird, but in English the word 'sparrow' calls up a vision of the dingy and quarrelsome chatterer of the London squares, and such is certainly not the most poetically appropriate locomotive power for the brilliant car of the foam-born goddess in her flight.... Even others of the sparrow tribe lack dignity, though there may have been a Lesbian bird which seemed suitable to Sappho. According to Liddell and Scott the word is used generally for a bird, and by Aeschylus even to mean an eagle; though usually a small bird is understood. Swan would perhaps be an appropriate, though perhaps not an exact, reading."

Compare translators—For a comparison of modern English language translators, Jeffrey Duban in *Ancient and Modern Images of Sappho* shows the diversity of translations of a single stanza of a poem of Sappho's, known as the *Hymn to Aphrodite* (See BB pp. 14–15, Duban, pp. 5–14).

French prose—Although most French translations of Sappho are rhymed, Meunier chose prose translation because: "Le sens du fond importe plus que les mots dont se revêt la forme ... sans les paraphraser et sans trop émousser le rhythme intime de leur élan lyrique, de les traduire. [The meaning is more important than words which duplicate the rhyme scheme ... without paraphrasing and without too much attentuating the internal rhythm of their lyric spirit, of their translating.]"

WHAT ENGLISH TRANSLATIONS OF SAPPHO WERE DONE?

1475 Commentary—Wharton: (170 fragments were known in 1895) "The British Museum contains a sort of commentary on Sappho which is dated 1475.... It is written in Latin by Georgius Alexandrinus Merula." "The first edition of any part of Sappho was that of the *Hymn to Aphrodite*, by H. Stephanus, in his edition of Anacreon, 8vo, 1554.... Vossius gave an emended text of the two principal odes in his edition of Catullus, London, 4vo, 1684."

Wolf, 1733—Wharton: "But the first separation edition of Sappho's works was that of Johann Christian Wolf, which was published in 4vo at Hamburg in 1733, and reprinted under an altered title two years later.... The next important critical edition of Sappho was that of Heinrich Friedrich Magnus Volger, 8vo, Leipzig, 1810."

Sapphic question—Wharton: "Nothing written before 1816 really grasped the Sapphic question. In that year Welcker published his celebrated refutation of the long-current calumnies against Sappho, Sappho vindicated from a prevailing prejudice. In his zeal to establish her character, he may have been here and there led in extravagance, but it is certain that his searching criticism first made it possible to appreciate her true position. Nothing that has been written since has succeeded in invalidating his main conclusions. ...Consequently the next self-standing edition of Sappho, by Christian Friedrich Neue, 4vo, Berlin, 1827, embodying the results of the 'new departure,' was far in advance of its predecessors ... in critical excellence."

WHAT IS SAPPHO'S PUBLICATION HISTORY?

Nine books—Meunier: "Sappho, it is said, wrote nine books of poetry. This distribution into nine books, probably given by the grammarians of Alexandria, was throughout founded on the nature of the meters and the types employed by Sappho. The first book was composed in sapphic strophes; one other in asclepiadean verse; a third in verse alkaic. We ignore thus the Epithalamiums, the Elegies and the Hymns formed also different books. Of all this, there only remains with us today a hundred sixty-two fragments.... It is not much, but it is however enough for us to be able to see what must be the poetry of Sappho."

BIBLIOGRAPHY

Bagg, R., "Love, Ceremony and Daydream in Sappho's Lyrics," *Arion*, Vol. 3 (1964), pp. 44-81.

Barnard, Mary. *Sappho: A New Translation*. Berkeley: University of California Press, 1958

Barnstone, Willis. *Greek Lyric Poetry*. New York: Schocken, 1962

Bascoul, F. *La chaste Sappho de Lesbos*, Paris, 1911.

Bergk, *Anthologia Lyrica*, 1914.

_____. *Poetae Lyrici Graeci*, t. III, 1932

Bowra, C.M. *Greek Lyric Poetry: From Alcman to Simonides*. Oxford: Oxford University Press, 1961, 1967.

Campbell, David A. *Greek Lyric, Vol. I. Sappho and Alcaeus,* Cambridge: Harvard University Press, 1982. Revised edition of Edmonds.

Carson, Anne. *Eros the Bittersweet*. Princeton: Princeton University Press, 1986

Cox, Edwin Marion. *The Poems of Sappho with Historical & Critical Notes, Translations, and a Bibliography*. New York: Charles Scribner's Sons, 1925.

Croiset, Alfred, *Histoire de la Littérature grecque*. Tr. as *An abridged history of Greek Literature*. New York: Macmillan, 1904.

Davenport, Guy. *Archilochos, Sappho, Alkman,* Berkeley: University of California Press, 1980.

Davison, John Armstrong. *From Archilochus to Pindar.* London: Macmillan, 1968

Demetrius. *Aristotle's Poetics; Demetrius, On Style.* New York: Dutton, 1934

Diehl, E. *Anthologia lyrica Graeca* I, Leipzig, 1935.

Dionysus of Halicarnassus. *On Literary Composition.* ed. & tr. W. Rhys Roberts. London: Macmillan, 1910.

Duban, Jeffrey M., *Ancient and Modern Images of Sappho, Translations and Studies in Archaic Greek Love Lyric*. Lanham: University Press of America, 1983

Edmonds, J.M. *The new fragments of Sappho*, Cambridge, 1909.

_____. *Lyra Graeca*. Vols. I-III. Cambridge: Harvard U. Press, 1922-52

Fränkel, Hermann. *Early Greek Poetry and Philosophy.* tr. Moses Hadas and James Willis. New York: Harcourt Brace Jovanovich, 1962.

Friedrich, P. *The Meaning of Aphrodite.* Chicago: University of Chicago Press, 1978.

Gerber, D.E. "Studies in Greek Lyric Poetry: 1967-1975," *The Classical World*, Vol. 70 (1976077), 65-157.

_____. "A Survey of Publications on Greek Lyric Poetry Since 1952," *The Classical World*, Vol. 61 (1967-68), 265-79, 317-30, 378-85.

Gentili, Bruno. *Poetry and Its Public in Ancient Greece.* tr. A. Thomas Cole. Baltimore: Johns Hopkins U. Press, 1988.

Groden, S.Q. *The Poems of Sappho.* New York: Bobbs-Merrill, 1966.

Haines, C.R. *Sappho, the Poems and Fragments.* London: Routledge, 1926.

Hall, John. "An uncommon little book." *Translation of the Height of Eloquence by Dionysius Longinus.* London: 1652. This includes the first known published English translation of a poem of Sappho.

Hallett, J.P. "Sappho and Her Social Context: Sense and Sensuality," *Signs: Journal of Women in Culture and Society*, Vol. 4 (1979), 447-64.

Johnson, Walter Ralph. *The Idea of Lyric.* Berkeley: University of California Press, 1982.

Kirkwood, G.M. *Early Greek Monody: The History of a Poetic Type.* Ithaca: Cornell U. Press, 1974.

_____. "A Survey of Recent Publications Concerning Classical Greek Lyric Poetry," *The Classical World*, Vol. 47 (1953-54), 33-42, 49-54.

Lattimore, Richmond. *Greek Lyrics.* Chicago: University of Chicago Press, 1949.

Lefkowitz, M.R. "Critical Stereotypes and the Poetry of Sappho," *Greek, Roman, and Byzantine Studies*, Vol. 14 (1973), 113-23.

Lobel, E. *The fragments of the lyrical poems of Sappho*, Oxford, 1925

Lobel, Edgar and Denys Page, *Poetarum Lesbiorum Fragmenta*, Oxford: Oxford U. Press, 1955.

Lorimer, H.L. *Homer and the Monuments.* London: Macmillan, 1950.

Menander. *Leukadias.* A two-page fragment in *The Principal Fragments,* tr. Francis G. Allinson. London: Heinemann, 1921.

Meunier, Mario. *Sappho, Anacréon et Anacréontiques.* Paris: Éditions Bernard Grasset, 1932.

_____. *Sappho, traduction nouvelle de tous les fragments connus, précédée d'une étude sur la poétesse de Lesbos.* 1911.

Miller, Marion Mills and David Moore Robinson. *The Songs of Sappho.* New York: Frank-Maurice, 1925.

Mora, Édith. *Sappho, histoire d'un poète et traduction intégrale de l'oeuvre.* Paris: Flammarion, 1966.

Muller, Otto. *Litterat. grecq.*

Mure, G.R.G. *History of greek literature*

Nagy, G. "Phaethon, Sappho's Phaon and the White Rock of Leukas," *Harvard Studies in Classical Philology*, vol. 77 (1973), 137-77.

Page, Denys L. *Sappho and Alcaeus: an Introduction to the Study of Ancient Lesbian Poetry.* Oxford; Clarendon Press, 1970.

Patrick, Mary Mills. *Sappho and the Island of Lesbos.* Boston: Houghton Mifflin, 1914

Philips, Ambrose. in *The Works of Anacreon and Sappho done from the Greek by several hands*, etc. London, 1713. 8 vols.

Powell, Jim. *Sappho, A Garland, The Poems and Fragments of Sappho.* tr. Jim Powell. New York: Farrar Straus Giroux, 1993

Reinach, Théodore with Aimé Puech. *Alcée Sapho.* Paris: Les Belles-Lettres, 1937, 1960.

Reinach, Théodore. *Pour mieux connaître Sappho*, Académie des Inscriptions et Belles Lettres, Compte rendu des Séances de 1911.

Robinson, D.M. *Sappho and Her Influence.* Boston: Marshall Jones, 1924.

Roche, P. *The Love Songs of Sappho.* New York: Mentor, 1966.

Sandre, Thierry. *Athénée*

Sappho. *Sappho.* in *Greek Lyrics*, tr. Richmond Lattimore. Chicago: University of Chicago Press, 1960.

_____. *Sappho.* tr. Mary Barnard, Berkeley: University of California Press, 1958.

_____. *Sappho.* in *Greek Lyric Poetry*, tr. Willis Barnstone. New York: Schocken Books, 1972

Stigers, E.S. "Romantic Sensuality, Poetic Sense: A Response to Hallett on Sappho," *Signs: Journal of Women in Culture and Society*, Vol. 4 (1979), 465-71.

_____. "Sappho's Private World," *Women's Studies*, Vol. 8 (1981), 47-63.

_____. "Sappho and the Enclosing Goddess," paper delivered at the Fifth Berkshire Conference, Vassar, June 1981.

Swinburne, Algernon Charles. in *The Saturday Review*, vol. 117 (1914) 228

Treu, Max. *Sappho, Greichisch und deutsch herausgegeben.* München: Hernst Heimeran Verlag, 1954.

Voigt, Eva Maria. *Sappho et Alcaeus.* Amsterdam: Polak & Van Gennep/ Atheneum, 1971.

Weigall, A. *Sappho of Lesbos: Her Life and Times.* New York: Frederick A. Stokes, 1932.

Welcker, Friedrich Gottlieb. *Kleine Schriften*

Wharton, H.T. *Sappho: Memoir, Text, Renderings, and a Literal Translation.* London: John Lane and Chicago: A.C. McClurg, 1887.

Wilamowitz, *Sappho und Simonides.* Berlin: Weidmann, 1966

Winkler, John J., *The Constraints of Desire.* New York: Routledge, 1990.

Glossary

Achilles: greatest Greek warrior at the siege of Troy

Aeolian: a branch of Greek-speaking peoples, settled on the west coast of Asia Minor from Troy south to the Hermus River, and neighboring islands

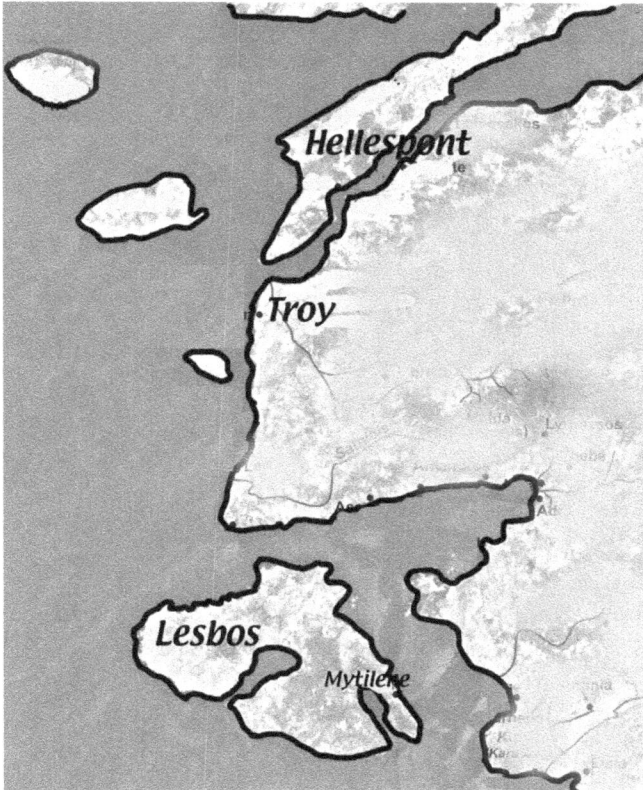

Agamemnon: Leader of the Greeks against the Trojans in the Trojan War

agora: town center, market place

Alexandria: Greek city established on the north coast of Egypt by Alexander the Great, center of Hellenistic culture

Alkaios: (c. 620 BCE) Lesbian political poet contemporary with Sappho

Anacreon: (c. 570–?? BCE)Ionian lyric poet from Teos; his themes are love and drink, his meters are not complex.

Anactoria: friend of Sappho

Anaximenes: (c. 546 BCE) Ionian philosopher who saw the origin of everything in the element of air

Andromache: daughter of King Eetion of Thebe, wife of Hector. She survived the fall of Troy and was given to Achilles' son Neoptolemus. She later married the Trojan Helenus.

Andromeda: rival of Sappho

Antipater of Sidon: (c. 120 BCE) Greek elegiac poet.

Aphrodite: Greek goddess of love and fertility, protector of sailors; Homer calls her "the Cyprian."

Archilochos: (c. 650 BCE) satiric Greek poet from Paros

Arion of Methymna: (c.650 BCE) Lesbian poet, student of Alkman, created the dithyramb, out of which Greek tragedy was born.

Aristarchos of Samothrace: (c.215–c.143 BCE) head of Alexandrian Library, and first to define scholarship, complete with notes, commentaries, critical editions

Aristocles: Born name of Plato, which is a nickname meaning flat or broad. Also, a ruler of Athens

Aristophanes: (c.445–c.385 BCE) Greek comic playwright and poet; eleven plays survive. His humor is parody and exaggeration, his bias is conservative, against the new cultural movements in Athens.

Aristophanes of Byzantium: (c.200 BCE) scholar, head of the famous Alexandrian Library

Aristotle: (384–322 BCE) Greek philosopher from Stageira, student of Plato, teacher of **Alexander the Great.** Aristotle emphasized definition, classification and analysis, the basis for modern science

Arnold, Edwin: English translator, author of *Light of Asia*

Aspasia: companion of Pericles, intellectual

Athenaeus: (c. 200 CE) Greek author of *Deipnosophistai—Dinner Talk of the Great,* an anecdotal source for Hellenistic manners and attitudes

Atthis: friend of Sappho

Attic Greek: Greek spoken in Athens

Bowra: C.M.: English classical scholar and translator

caesura: mid-way pause in a poetic line

Catullus: (c.84–c.54 BCE) Roman poet, imitator of Sappho; his poetry is racy but erudite

Charaxos: brother of Sappho

choriamb: poetic foot of - ˘ ˘ -, long-short-short-long

chorus: Greek theatrical device, usually a group replying or speaking in unison

cithara: large lyre

Cleis: Mother of Sappho; daughter of Sappho

Cleobulina: riddle poet

Demetrius of Phalerum: (c.350–c.283 BCE) Athenian pro-Macedonian politiican; helped found Alexandrian Library

digamma: obsolete Greek letter, resembling *F*, with the sound of *w*

Dodona: ancient oracle of Zeus in Epirus

Dionysius of Halicarnassus: (c.30 BCE) Greek historian and critic

Diotima: mentor of Socrates

Doricha: slave freed by Charaxos; Herodotus calls this woman Rhodopis (rose-faced)

epithalamium: (*at the bedroom*) wedding song

Eresos: perhaps the birthplace of Sappho

Erinna: poet, possibly a student of Sappho's

Eurygius: a brother of Sappho

Eustathius: (c.1150 CE) Commentator on ancient Greek texts

foot: poetic foot, rhythmic segment of a line of poetry

Gorgo: rival of Sappho

gynécée: *See* women's room

Hector: son of King Priam of Troy, and battle leader during the Siege

Helen: wife of Menelaus, fled with Paris to Troy, the incident that caused the Trojan War

Hephaistion of Alexandria: (c.150 BCE) Greek writer on metrics, source of many quotes

Hermes: god who, among other things, led the recently deceased to Hades

Hermogenes of Tarsus: (c.160 CE) Greek writer on literary style

Hesiod: (c.700 BCE) Greek epic poet, born in Boeotia; he brought everyday life to the epic style.

hetaera: woman dedicated to the service of Aphrodite; in later times the meaning changed to courtesan or prostitute. Many hetaerae were highly educated, an opportunity not available to wives in most of Greece.

Himerius: (c.310–c.390) born in Bithynia. Greek rheotrician.

Hipponax of Ephesus: (c.550 BCE) Greek earthy satiric poet; invented parody and the "limping iambic foot"

Homer: (c.750 BCE) Greek epic poet. Homer's *Iliad* and *Odyssey* were important parts of Greek education.

hymenaeus: marriage song sung to the bride on her way to the groom's house, usually invoking a "god of marriage" called Hymen; there are no temples or records of such a god except in these songs.

Ionia: Greek settlements in Asia Minor from Smyrna to Miletus, and nearby islands; birthplace of Greek philosophy. Much of the Ionian migration must have come through Athens.

ithyphallic: of an erect penis; the ithyphallus was a monstrous construction paraded in festivals of Dionysus.

Kerkolas: husband of Sappho

Korinna: (c.525 BCE) lyric poet from Boeotia, teacher of Pindar

Larichos: brother of Sappho

Lattimore, Richmond: classical scholar and translator

Lesbos: large island off Asia Minor

Lesches: Greek poet, anuthor of the *Little Iliad*, sequel to Homer's *Iliad*

Longinus: The Greek essay *On the Sublime*, signed by "Dionysius Longinus," was formerly attributed to Cassius Longinus, but now is considered of unknown date and author—who is often called "pseudo-Longinus." Nevertheless, the essay's wit, breadth of learning, and quotations (including one from the Hebrew Bible), make it a valuable resource.

Louÿs, Pierre: author of *Songs of Bilitis*, a romance of Sappho's school.

lyre: a harp-like stringed instrument, with little or no soundbox, and no frets

magadis: type of lyre

Maximus of Tyre: (c.580–662) known as "the Confessor"

Menelaus: husband of Helen, brother of Agamemnon

Mixolydian: musical scale, corresponding to B to B on the white keys of a piano

Myrtis: poet of Boeotia, teacher of Korinna and perhaps Pindar

Mytilene: capital of Lesbos

Naucratis: Greek port settlement in the Nile Delta in Egypt, famous for prostitutes

oikia mousopolon: house of poets

Orpheus: Pre-Homeric poet legendized; he helped the Argonauts escape the Sirens, his music could move trees and rocks. Poems atributed to him describe mystery rites.

Ovid: Publius Ovidius Naso (43 BCE–17 CE) Roman poet. In his *Heroides*, he includes the possibly apochryphal story of Sappho and Phaon.

Oxyrynchus papyrus: an early twentieth-century find in Upper Egypt which includes previously unknown lines and fragments from Sappho.

Pericles: (c.495–429 BCE) Greek statesman supporting democracy; he dominated Athenian politics for thirty years, including the conversion of the Delian League into the Athenian Empire, precipitating war with Sparta. In peacetime he promoted building sculpture and the Parthenon.

Phryne: (c.350 BCE) Greek hetaera from Boeotia; she was a model for still-existing sculptures by Apelles and Praxiteles

Pindar: (518–c.446 bce) Greek poet of odes and choral lyrics, born in Boeotia

Pittakos: (c.650–c.570) Lesbian statesman, one of the Seven Sages of Greece. He was elected dictator for ten years to restore order, during which time he reformed the laws. He then relinquished power to retire.

Plato: (427–347 BCE) Greek philosopher and writer; colleague of Socrates, founder of Idealism

Plutarch: (c.46–c.120 CE) Greek biographer and historian, author of *Parallel Lives,* pairing Greek and Roman historical figures

Pnyx: hill just west of the Acropolis where the Athenian assembly met, and citizens discussed issues

polysyndeton: repetitive use of conjunctions

Posidippos: (c.250 BCE) Greek New Comedy dramatist

Pythian oracle: Pythian priestess of Apollo at the oracle of Delphi

Rhodopis: slave freed by Charaxos; Sappho names her Doricha in her poem

sapphics: rhythmic pattern used by Sappho and Alkaios

Sardis: capital of Lydia

Scamandronymos: Sappho's father

scolia: short songs sung by each guest in turn at a dinner party—the singer holds a myrtle bough while singing and passes it on for the next verse. Terpander originated the scolion.

Servius: (c. 425 CE) Marius Servius Honoratus, Latin grammarian.

Simonides of Ceos: (556–468 BCE) Greek poet famous for his epitaphs

slavery: involuntary servitude; slaves in Greece often had been prisoners of war.

Socrates: (469–339 BCE) Greek philosopher; self-styled "gadfly" of Athens

Stesichoros: (*choirmaster*) (c.575 BCE) Original name Teisias. Greek poet born at Mataurus, lived in Sicily. He wrote choral lyrics on a wide range of epic stories.

Strabo: (64 BCE–?24 ce) Greek geographer and historian, born in Amasia, Pontus

Symonds, John Addington: English critic

Syrianus: Neoplatonist philosopher in Athens c.450 CE.

Telesilla: (c.450 BCE) Greek poet, famous for arming the Argive women after Sparta defeated the men of Argos

Terpander: (c.650 BCE) Lesbian musician and poet, inventor of the cithara, a seven-stringed lyre. He wrote *nomes* (melodies for epic set pieces), scolia, and introductions to epics.

Thales: (c.600 BCE) Greek philosopher and scientist

Thaletas: Cretan poet who lived in Sparta. He wrote paeans and festival dance-songs

thiasos: a quasi-religious 'college'; a band, group, or association

women's room: An area in Greek households set aside for women; a harem. In most of Greece these rooms served as social arena for women, who were not afforded the same privileges and public institutions as men for social interaction.

www.ingramcontent.com/pod-product-compliance
Lightning Source LLC
Chambersburg PA
CBHW021345090426
42742CB00008B/753